stories of triumph

WOMEN

WHO

WIN

in sport and in life

PHOTOGRAPHY and INTERVIEWS by CHRISTINA LESSA

FOREWORDS by PEGGY FLEMING and PICABO STREET

AFTERWORD BY TERESA EDWARDS

UNIVERSE

WITH SINCERE THANKS

CHARLES MIERS *for the opportunity to work with universe again.* ALEX TART *for saving the day again and again.* BONNIE ELDON *because she works so hard.* MR. LENNY @ SOMETHING SPECIAL *for all the faxes and bagels.* BRIAN and NEIL @ CRC LAB, NYC *for the beautiful imagery.* SARA HALL and ERIC ZONE *for all the great advice.* DEBRA GOLDSTEIN *for getting the ball rolling.* BOB SCHNECK *for letting me borrow his protégé and supporting the arts once again.* REEBOK *for the soccer balls.* NIKE *for the beautiful jerseys.* THE WOMEN'S SPORTS FOUNDATION *for the contacts and the amazing contributions to society.* PEGGY FLEM-ING *for making time for this project and* SUE LIPTON *for helping her make time.* BEN GIOVE *for being a nice guy.* SUE RODIN @ STARS & STRATEGIES *for being a kind and dedicated agent.* PETER MOSCONI @ VILLA MOSCONI, NYC *for being so patient.* RUSSELL WALKER, CAPTAIN LIFEGUARD, BAYWATCH, LOS ANGELES, *for a great day on the boat.* JOHN STUDINER, ASSER LEVY POOL, NYC *for keeping the lap swimmers at bay for a few more minutes.* LAUREN KAPLAN, PUBLIC RELATIONS, CHELSEA PIERS, NYC *for use of the sky rink.* STEVEN PERFIDIA, @ PATRICIA FIELD, NYC *for the great retro hair on jenny thompson.* FRANCESCO RIZZA @ BANCO DI ROMA *for keeping the funds flowing.* KAREN BARTSCH-DiMEGLIO, and DIANA MCUGH, DELTA AIRLINES *for getting us on the red-eye to los angeles.* JULIE, MATT, and PETER RABBIT *just because.* J.J. *for being a great assistant.* PAT McCORMICK ENTERPRISES *for doing so much for children.* LISA HICKMAN. MEGAN, SERENA, BRIAN MACINTIRE, AMY BARRET @ BURTON SNOWBOARDS. MARILYN CRAWFORD. JONATHAN LESSA and SASHA CHUDNOVSKY *for being great godparents.* MR. and MRS. FERNANDEZ *for letting me into their home.* TOM McCARTHY. BOB KERSEE. SHADE GLOBAL. RAHN TOBLER. AMERICA TRUE³. ERIC TRIEBACH. DEBBIE ZEALLY @ ADVANTAGE INTERNATIONAL, NADIA GUERRIERO @ GOLD MEDAL MANAGEMENT. WILDCARD GYM. MIKE BURG and THE TOM COLLINS TOUR. ABS. NORMA KAMALI. ANDREA FRANKOSKI *for the great ideas.* MY SIX GUARDIAN ANGELS *especially "auntie" frannie.* DARLING OWEN and BABY JAKE *for your patience and love.* MOM and DAD. DAN PETRUCELLI *for everything.*

MARY LESSA *wardrobe styling*, DANA YORIO *hair and make-up*

IN MEMORY OF DEAR AUNTIE "M"

ADDITIONAL IMAGERY COURTESY OF: TOM SERVAIS (p. 40); BARBARA LIVINGSTON (p. 56); MIKE POWELL/ALLSPORT (p. 120, 122–3); TONY NESTE (p. 128); STEVE REYES (p. 132–3)

First published in the United States of America in 1998 by UNIVERSE PUBLISHING, a division of Rizzoli International Publications, Inc. 300 Park Avenue South, New York, NY 10010

© 1998 by Christina Lessa   Produced by CD Productions, New York, NY   Design by Dan Petrucelli

98 99 00 01 02 / 10 9 8 7 6 5 4 3 2 1   Printed in England   Library of Congress Catalog Card Number: 98-61420

CONTENTS

Things were a lot different for female athletes in 1968. We were seen, but rarely heard, and we were encouraged to keep our opinions to ourselves. That year on February 10, I won my gold medal in figure skating in Grenoble, France. At the time I didn't realize that my participation in the sport would be considered groundbreaking. I also had no idea how it would change my life.

In 1961, the entire U.S. figure skating team died in a plane crash on the way to the world championships. I was only eleven and unaware of the gap that this would create in our sport on a national level. Because all my potential role models were gone, I had to draw on inspiration from what I had seen of ballet, music, and art. I had to look inside myself for what I thought my style should be.

I was told I moved very differently from the skaters who had come before me, that it seemed so natural and effortless. It wasn't. It took a tremendous amount of work and dedication to achieve what I wanted to express on the ice, but I loved what I was doing. By creating a unique style, I hope I've opened up doors for other skaters to do the same. I'm very flattered when I'm referred to as a "feminine" skater. Elegance and grace are what I have always admired in women, no matter what their profession, and I'm proud to have brought that side of my personality to my sport.

I believe that we owe it to the women of the future to encourage young girls to express themselves through sports. Sports are not just a display of athletic power; they are a tool to help develop self-esteem and a healthy image. They also teach respect for discipline and responsibility. *Women Who Win* offers portraits of the kinds of role models needed to guide young female athletes in a positive direction, not only on the playing field but also in life.

Thirty years, to the day, after winning my Olympic gold medal, I was faced with another challenge: surgery for breast cancer. Once again, I had to call on all the lessons my sport had taught me: strength, confidence, and focus. Just as those lessons carried me to an Olympic title, they now are steering me toward a bright, healthy future. The impact my sport has had on my life continues to amaze me, and I am very, very grateful for the journey.

I'm proud to be included in this remarkable team of women—twenty-two successful athletes who perform at the highest levels of our sports, some of which are pretty extreme—and to be part of the documentation of the beginning of an era. But it is especially rare and wonderful to be portrayed in the photographs and text as a person, not just an athlete, which is a real switch from the usual sports portrait. I'm glad to show people that there is more to me than a ski outfit and an action shot. A lot of female athletes are concerned about the manner in which they're photographed. We have the confidence of world-class athletes, but get us behind closed doors and we struggle with insecurities just like anyone else. The audience that reads this book will see us in a different light and hear us in our own voices.

When I flipped through my mom's yearbook, it struck me that there was not a single team available for her to be on. So—wow—the women's movement in sports has come a long, long way. There's much more competition, but at the same time there are many new opportunities. By raising standards for women in sports, I believe we've helped to change women's perception of what is good health. There are still plenty of women out there who don't take care of themselves, but there are many more athletic women now, and we're putting more time into our bodies and our general health.

I don't think that there should be a lot of competition between men and women. We are completely different in the way we think, feel, function, desire, and make decisions. Our chemical makeup is different. While I sometimes envy the way men can put their emotions on the back burner, I think one of the great strengths of women is that they are better able to bring them to the surface. In doing so, women in sports develop their whole selves and can grow as athletes and people at the same time. Some people think of me as kind of a super hero and then I go blow myself apart and show that I am extremely human. So it has been important for me to have a connection to the people who watch me and for them to realize that I make mistakes and get hurt and feel sad sometimes, just like them. In general, I think, women in sports are more concerned about making that kind of connection with their fans. We feel a sense of responsibility to them and I think that is one of the most important contributions from women to this generation and those to come. I hope that, as competition among women continues to grow fiercer and more women enter the sports world as top competitors, we don't lose sight of our responsibilities and our abilities to be role models for other women as well as for men. We should push ourselves to athletic extremes in what we do, but never let that warp us as people.

When I was in grade school, the United States government adopted legislation called Title IX, which prohibited gender discrimination in federally funded schools and other institutions. It was 1972, and Little League for girls was about to become all the rage. The "sandpit," as we called it, would never again be the place where my girlfriends and I would go to buy penny candy and see if we could catch the attention of some popular boys while looking as cool as possible. From then on, it would be a place to go and see whose parents (very few at the time) had allowed their daughter to join and if she was any good. There was no question that I wouldn't be joining the lucky few: "What if the ball hits you in the face, or, even worse, the pelvis, rendering you infertile? Who will marry you?," my parents asked. This anxiety was the usual response to any pastime that seemed unladylike: the trumpet (they feared I'd get a cleft lip), the drums (they didn't want me to get big arms), soccer (oh, those unsightly knee scars!), and so on. No, my parents weren't interested in me becoming a child bride, in fact, they were very enthusiastic about education, encouraging me all the way through my master's degree. The issue of girls playing sports wasn't theirs alone, and it wasn't really based on capability; it was the state of society. When it was time for gym class, all the girls, with the exception of one or two "jocks" (whom we secretly envied, but publicly considered sort of sexless), would clamor for an excuse to not participate for fear of embarrassment. We worried about looking fat in our uniforms and boys making fun of us. At the time, no one cared if we were athletic or not, as long as we looked good.

But there was a period before our self-consciousness crept in—that priceless time during childhood when you can become both an astronaut and Miss America at the same time. You are unaware of the ways of the world and understand without question that your body and mind are useful and strong, capable and reliable. The women in this book have fought to maintain this innocent ideal. Although they come from different backgrounds, their stories are tales of triumphing over the loss of oneself; they have learned to be undaunted by ridicule and challenged by adversity. These athletes share the common desire to brighten the future for those who will follow in their footsteps. Nearly all of them have created a foundation or charity on their own, with a sense of dedication that is uniquely female.

Women have always struggled with issues of femininity and athleticism. It's a physical thing, too, as Jenny Thompson stated. She was not always confident in her appearance: "Are my arms too big, too ugly?" But after much reflection she realized, "My arms are what make me swim so fast and they're part of who I am." It's also an issue of character. Is someone like Missy Giove misunderstood because of her alternative looks and aggressive, no-nonsense behavior? Sheryl Swoopes wants women to know that it's okay to be strong and still go to the mall. This seems funny, but as any woman who has ventured into a male-dominated field knows, one's every move is being scrutinized by those who feel that women can't be both strong and feminine (not to mention attractive) at the same time. Fortunately, old-school beliefs are fading, and with developments such as the establishment of the WNBA and the ABL in 1996, the United States Olympic women's hockey team in 1998, and women's World Cup soccer in 1999, the new millennium looks like it's going to offer a different world to young women interested in sports.

The athletes I have chosen for this project represent a broad range of humanity. Some are old enough to remember the Billie Jean King/Bobby Riggs match as if it were yesterday. Others have just started their careers in sports that are less than a decade old. The common thread between all of these tremendous athletes is not only their talent and drive for success, but an understanding of what it is to be a woman in what was traditionally a man's world. When Julie Krone became intent on becoming a jockey as a teenager, she could only imagine the struggle that was ahead. She had to make her mark in the only professional sport (other than race car driving) in which she would not only be dominated by the number of men, but she would be competing against them as well. Even Shannon Dunn, a competitor in the modern sport of snowboarding, must struggle to get the same attention as her male counterparts. However, the fact of the matter is that all of these opportunities are gifts, and though it's a constant challenge, these women have all made the most of what life has given them. Prior to Title IX, approximately 300,000 girls played interscholastic sports across the nation. Twenty-five years later, that figure has leapt to approximately 2.25 million.

At a recent family gathering, my mother asked my young cousin what she wanted to be when she grew up. "A professional soccer player," she replied. It occurred to me at that moment that today, this is a real option for her, not just a fantasy, and she really meant it. When I interviewed fifteen-year-old Tara Lipinski, she seemed unfazed by the novelty of professional female athletes; it's something that she simply expects as a normal part of life. For athletes closer to my generation, such as Julie Foudy from the U.S. women's soccer team, it's a dream that has come to fruition only after years of knowing that their career choice was a gamble. The true pioneers, Shirley Muldowney included, competed against men because there were no other women and lived through the pain and struggle of creating a new path for others to follow. Shirley is still at the top of her field after forty years, yet finds it almost impossible to attract significant sponsorship: "No one wants to sponsor an old lady, even if she is holding the top speed record." The issue of support, both financial and emotional, is an important one for women in sports. Not only are most women paid less than men in their sports, many of them have to hold second and third jobs to support themselves. But money is not the main issue in women's sports, as it has come to be with a lot of men's. The main issue is team spirit. There is a tremendous sense of camaraderie among the players, as well as the fans—women from all walks of life. It's about the love of the games and a celebration of freedom. When women in sports achieve victory, it's a celebration for everyone: the homemaker, the movie star, the wanna-bes, and the next generation.

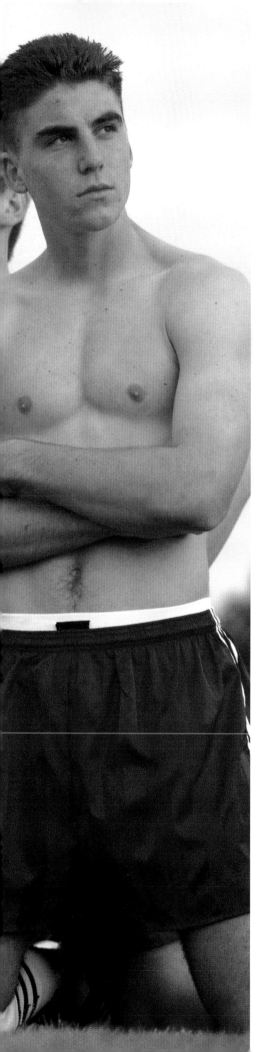

FOUDY

co-captain, olympic gold-medal-winning soccer team, 1996
winner, f.i.f.a. fair play award, 1997
four-time all-american

Her agent warns me: "Julie hates photo shoots, so if you want to make her happy, bring doughnuts." We search in vain for a doughnut shop along the way. I arrive empty-handed and nervous. But Julie Foudy has a generous spirit. She jumps out of her car and unloads several dozen soccer balls for the shoot. She puts her hand on my shoulder and tells me how happy she is to be involved in such a great project. She makes me and everyone else around her feel so comfortable—like old friends. Just as we finish, a group of young girls converges on the field to practice. They spot Julie and rush over for an autograph. She goes one better and donates the balls to their team.

In most parts of the world, men's soccer is an obsession. But the most renowned spectator sport in the world didn't become prevalent in the United States until the mid-seventies. From that point on, all over America, soccer was as popular with the girls as it was with the boys.

I had an idea that in other parts of the world it wasn't as acceptable for girls to participate in sports—in some places, it was even taboo—but I had never experienced it firsthand. It wasn't until I was sixteen, traveling to compete in other countries, that I realized that other girls didn't have the luxury or opportunity to play in organized leagues. I was in between tournaments in Spain and wanted to stay in shape so I started to practice with some local men. Every time we played, a crowd would gather to watch—not because we were superstars, but because they had never seen a woman playing with men.

While playing a disorganized and underfunded women's national team in Brazil in 1993, we were literally mocked and sworn at by the predominantly male fans. It was painful. But I don't think it's too idealistic to say that, one day, soccer won't be a gender-specific sport. In three years Brazil has changed drastically. The government now pours money into the women's team, as it always has with the men's team. In 1997 we lost to them for the first time.

I DIDN'T PLAY FOR MY FOLKS;
MY PASSION CAME FROM WITHIN, NOT FROM SOME EXTERNAL SOURCE.
I BELIEVE THAT'S THE REASON WHY I'M STILL PLAYING
AFTER TWENTY YEARS—BECAUSE I PLAY FOR ME.

I think that's why the U.S. women's team is so successful—because we never had the cultural taboos to overcome. Sports were a large part of my childhood. No one in my family played soccer (although to this day my brothers insist that they taught me everything I know), but it became my sport of choice, and at age seven I started with the Mission Viejo Soccerettes in Southern California. I played on that team with the same group of girls for ten years, through high school.

i have always wanted to speak out for those who couldn't speak for themselves — especially children. and when you have a gold medal around your neck, people want to hear what you have to say. this opportunity is also a responsibility. this is when you can use your success to give back, to change the world.

My parents were very supportive but at the same time very noncommittal. This was really the key to my success. There were other parents who went to every game, as if their lives depended on their children being successful at soccer. I find that to be a big problem with youth athletics; parents push and push until eventually their child burns out. I didn't. In fact, I begged my mom to let me play soccer, but she said I had to wait until I was seven. It was an agonizing year. In second grade, I went out to play with the boys. My brothers' friends called me Jimmy because I used to walk around without my shirt on. Magic Johnson and Joe Montana were my role models. But I never felt like an oddball because of my parents' support.

I think the corporate world has finally realized the marketability of women's sports. But along with these opportunities comes more responsibility. We soccer players had heard about a problem in Pakistan—about children being employed to make soccer balls. There was a buzz about it. Believe it or not, the majority of soccer balls in the world are made in Pakistan. Each panel is still hand-sewn and an entire ball takes four hours to assemble. Unfortunately, for all of this labor there is little compensation. So when Reebok asked me to be a spokeswoman for their new line of soccer balls, I wanted to know specifically what Reebok was doing. I went to Pakistan myself and found out that the ball panels were being taken home by workers and their children were doing the stitching—the more balls assembled, the more money earned. So Reebok quickly took steps to remedy the problem. All of the stitching is now done on a single site, and human-rights activists are closely monitoring the situation. In addition, Reebok has started a school for the nine- to fourteen-year-olds who might otherwise be used as child labor. Now I'm prepared to be a spokesperson for the ball.

I couldn't imagine how different my life would be without athletics in it, which is not to say I live for sports. I do many things outside athletics; you have to have other interests, an education—the whole package. But it has been a blessing to see the world and to be able to make a living as a professional athlete. I'm fortunate—only a handful of the players on the national team can play without taking a second job, which we all used to do. I look toward the day when it is not a few handfuls but a hundred handfuls and women can play and work in the sport they love. It is a slow process, but in the ten years that I've played, it has been accelerating at match speed.

i wonder how many women out there have the potential

and the capability to do what i've done but have gone through life

without the support system to make it a reality. it makes me cringe to think of

parents telling girls that they shouldn't play sports because it's not an attractive thing

to do and they should be doing feminine things.

sometimes when women meet me in person they say,

"wow, i thought you'd be huge and really muscular."

they think, "maybe i can do it, maybe it's not such an

intangible goal." suddenly that intangible goal becomes realistic.

EDWARDS

the most decorated player in women's basketball
the only four-time u.s. basketball olympian
three-time winner, u.s.a. basketball's female athlete of the year

Teresa Edwards's shoot was less than perfect. The flight was overbooked, the limo was late, the address was wrong, hotel reservations were lost, and my twelve-foot ladder didn't fit in my ten-foot rental van. Sometimes it happens—a bad day—but Teresa was not only a good sport, she agreed to my every photographic whim and answered all of my questions without even a pause to wonder. Her discipline inspired me. "Christina, I see what you're trying to do, and we're going to do whatever it takes to get it done." It was obvious that getting the job done was this tremendous athlete's theme. Among her many accomplishments, Edwards played an instrumental role in the formation of the American Basketball League, and after two years with the Atlanta Glory (playing and coaching), she joined the Philadelphia Rage in the fall of 1998.

Basketball has always been the thrill of my life. As a child, I was a natural athlete. In most sports I held my own, but in basketball I flew. I didn't choose basketball; I believe it chose me. I know God gave this gift to me, and I use it to the best of my ability every day. Basketball is my drug; it feeds me and gives me everything I need. I get a high out of passing, shooting, outrunning my opponents, playing defense. Right now my life is surrounded by it, and I pray that my future will be too. I'm trying to do the best that I can while I'm here, and after this life is over and I have to answer to God, we will both know that giving back has been most important to me. He has his own plan for all of us, and that includes the arena of women's sports. I do feel that women's time on the playing field has come. It's a new day for sports, and it's a great day.

I grew up in a small town in Georgia called Cairo, a southern town where everyone knows everyone else. It was a nice place to grow up slow; I'm in my thirties and it still hasn't changed. I'm the oldest of five and the only girl. My brothers and I all played together, creating whatever we could think of. When you don't have a lot of money you become inventors. We'd make drums out of cardboard and have parades in the street. People would watch us from their porches and laugh. In my mind I can still hear and see these things. It was a good childhood.

When you come from a small town it's hard to realize that the same opportunities exist for you as for everyone else, so you can really get stuck. You have to make your own opportunities happen. It became my goal to inspire others and to be an example. I wanted to let kids know that they needed to get out and see the world. If kids could see the world's different cultures—even just the different cultures in the United States—they might want more out of life, to go beyond their local boundaries. I'm fortunate—somehow I made it out of there. I became successful at basketball, but not many other kids have followed me and that makes me sad because I always try to be a role model, a positive influence, a leader.

I DIDN'T CHOOSE BASKETBALL—
BASKETBALL CHOSE ME.
I KNOW GOD GAVE THIS GIFT TO ME
AND I USE IT TO THE BEST
OF MY ABILITY EVERY DAY. basketball is my drug—it fee
outrunning my opponents, playing defense. right now my life is surrounded by
to answer to God, we will both know that giving back h

...and gives me everything i need. i get a high out of passing, shooting,
...trying to do the best that i can while i'm here, and after this life is over, and i have
...en most important to me.

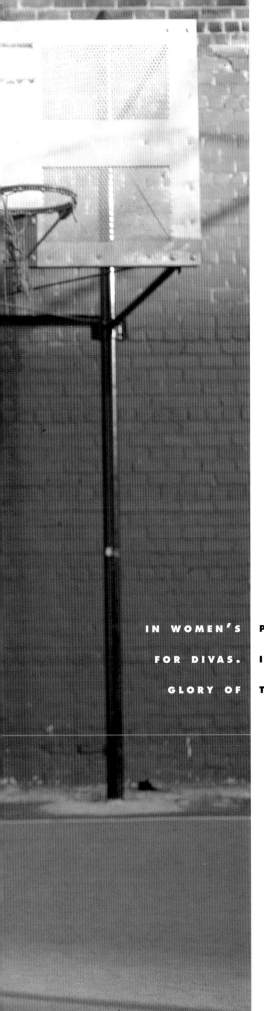

You have to be well-rounded. A lot of great male athletes from Cairo would get into good colleges on athletic scholarships, but they didn't do their homework. After the first semester they would find they couldn't maintain the academic requirements, or didn't realize the importance of those classes, and they would return home. It was sad because they were great athletes. When I got my scholarship, my mother and I went to sign together for the press to take pictures. She went to work the next day and the women that she worked with said, "Teresa will be back, just like the rest of them." It really hurt her to hear them say that. She always taught me to do my best and instilled in me a sense of pride. The one thing I didn't want to do was embarrass my mother.

My mother has been the biggest influence in my life. She did what she had to do to raise us as a single parent and never complained about her life. That helped me to maintain my focus throughout my education, and I loved basketball so much that I wasn't going to let anything jeopardize my chances. I never considered myself to be the smartest kid, so it was really about putting in the time.

IN WOMEN'S PROFESSIONAL SPORTS, THERE'S NO ROOM FOR DIVAS. IT'S ABOUT BLOOD, SWEAT, AND TEARS. BASKING IN THE GLORY OF THE GREATS—THAT'S THE GLAMOUR IN SPORTS.

People will gossip, especially in a small town. After college I started to play overseas and make some money—not much, but more than I had ever had in my life. I knew my mother needed a car. I couldn't afford a new car so I bought her a used car. All people back home could say was, "Why didn't Teresa buy her a house?" They were just people being people, but for me it was a motivation. I worked liked a dog to buy her the house we always dreamt of buying.

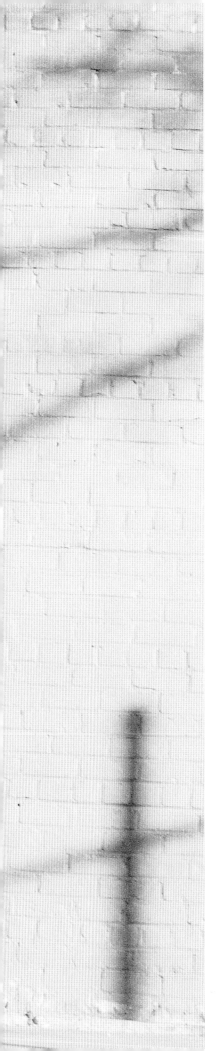

Once I realized that I was a role model, it became my goal to inspire others and to be an example. When you succeed, people want to be like you—that's what being a role model entails. You're out there and your every move is being watched. It is a fortunate situation in that it puts money in your pocket but unfortunate in that you are expected to be perfect. I don't mind being a role model if I am allowed to be human. I am going to make mistakes just like the next person.

I believe the real role models are not celebrities but the people kids grow up around everyday—parents, older siblings, teachers, doctors. Society doesn't want to acknowledge that, because it brings the burden of responsibility home.

If you really love the game, you don't get caught up in who's getting what. Dr. J and Pistol Pete got their due. It was late—but they got it. The payoff is being able to play and get paid for it. It's the reward for sticking it out through so many obstacles. I'm thirty-three and still here on the court, that's a joy in itself. I've been called a legend in women's basketball, and I'm alive to see it.

It's impossible to describe the feeling that this gives you. I feel that giving, not just taking from the sport, has made my life worth living. I don't spend my time looking back yet. There is still so much that I'd like to do. I'm still busy trying to succeed. Even when I'm old and can't move anymore I'll still be able to go to a game and watch the families exude pride over their little girls and know that I had something to do with it.

PAT & KELLY

McCORMICK

pat mccormick: four-time olympic gold medalist,
springboard and platform diving, 1952 and 1956

daughter kelly robertson: olympic bronze medalist, springboard diving, 1988
olympic silver medalist, springboard diving, 1984

Pat McCormick is sixty-eight years old, but within the first few minutes of following her around, I could barely keep up. Her office is lined with vintage pictures and clippings, including Pat posing as the first woman on the cover of Sports Illustrated *and an unbelievable publicity shot taken in 1952 of Pat diving off a shoddy plank four stories high into a small tub of water at Rockefeller Center. It's no wonder she continually amazed judges by performing dives previously attempted only by men.*

I competed in the 1956 Olympic trials just four months after giving birth to my first child, and at the time, women just didn't do those things. I could hardly find a doctor to support me. I made the team and we went to Australia, where my first event was on the three-meter. It was one of those events that you dream about—I couldn't do anything wrong. I won the event and was so far ahead in the competition. With three gold medals, I had one more event to go in the preliminary dives for a double-double (two diving gold medals in two Olympic Games). I followed the Russian gal in the ten-meter platform. I focused in, took hold of the edge of the towers, and kicked my handstand up—I was so aware of holding it. I held it so long I missed the dive. It put me in fourth place with two final dives left the following day.

I remember going back to the village and crying, wondering why I missed one of my strong dives. I really wanted my husband, Glen, to tell me how great I was and that I could do it. But he was the Olympic coach. The gal that was in first place was my roommate and teammate. He would never tell me anything different from what he was telling her, which I really respected. The next morning I woke up full of fear. All I could think of was that I had trained for fifteen years and I had two dives left that would take four seconds. When I walked up the steps I could see the whites of my knuckles. I got to the top, took my ready position, and took off. It had to be the very best dive of my life. I got back up to the top of the tower for my final dive, took my ready position, and took off again. I remember spinning it, dropping it, and getting what we call a rip injury. But when I popped up, I heard 10, 9.5, and 10. I'll never forget stepping up on the victory stand and reaching out for that fourth gold medal. The flag went up with the light shimmering on the water, and I realized I'd really reached my dream of winning those four gold medals.

I was born in 1930 in Seal Beach, California, on the second floor of a grocery store. My mother raised three kids by herself. She was the biggest influence on my life, but my biggest hero was my father, Robert Kelley. He was a decorated soldier in World War I. He had been shell-shocked, mustard-gassed, and had a hole in his foot that he received while he was fighting. He always told me to never be afraid of being the best. They found him dead in 1956 on skid row and the only thing that they found on his body were my clippings. That's how they identified him. One thing that I really admired about my mother is that she allowed me to continue to make him my hero. She never said a bad word about him.

I was a tomboy, always trying to keep up with my brother. I remember playing football when I was ten years old. I threw a pass and somebody said, "block that dame." I was completely wiped out—honest to goodness—because it was the first time I realized I was a girl. Girls didn't play football back then, and I went crying to my brother.

I'LL NEVER FORGET STEPPING UP ONTO THE VICTORY STAND AND REACHING OUT FOR THAT FOURTH GOLD MEDAL. THE FLAG WENT UP WITH THE LIGHT SHIMMERING ON THE WATER, AND I REALIZED I REALLY REACHED MY DREAM. *the pride i felt for myself and for my country has been one of the biggest gifts of my entire life.*

My brother suggested we go to a pier-to-pier swim, where they had a women's division. In a pier-to-pier swim, you swim two or three miles from one pier to another out in the ocean. It was my first competition and I took second place. I have to admit there were only two people in the race but I learned that the bigger the prize, the bigger the price.

My brother and I used to compete every Friday at the local Bay Shore Little Meets—swimming, diving, hopscotch. We just loved to compete— it didn't matter which place we took. Somebody saw me jumping on a springboard and asked if I would like to go up to the L.A. Athletic Club and try out for the diving team. I remember finding out that the pool was on the sixth floor and thinking that was a big deal. There, I met Sammy Lee and Vicki Draves, who had each won two Olympic gold medals in diving.

They were my mentors and they still are. I have wonderful videos of Sammy Lee saying when he first saw me that he thought I'd never make it. I don't think I was the most natural athlete in the world but I refused to lose. Mickey Mantle and I used to get together and wonder why we were so fortunate to be the winners when other people have the same ability. I don't know if it's because I have that extra drive or that extra focus. I just think it was something that I really wanted.

I could only afford one bathing suit a year, but I felt very blessed to have had the opportunity. I never dreamed of the responsibility that went along with being a gold medalist. I don't think you're really aware of the influence you have on others. My mother said once, "If you don't use what God has given you to help others it will be used against you." I think I'm beginning to understand that now. In 1984 I was on the Olympic organizing committee and my job was to give talks to schoolchildren. After my first talk, a teacher said to me, "A hundred kids here aren't going to make it." They were termed "at risk." I said, "I don't know what I can do, I'm not a teacher. Give me twenty-five kids and I'll give you two mornings a week." I started bringing in great role models like Rafer Johnson, an Olympic gold medalist in the decathlon, Paul Gonzalez, an Olympic gold medalist in boxing who grew up surrounded by gangs in the inner city. I took the kids to black-tie dinners, I took them to El Toro where my nephew was flying F18s. We started working on a little mantra: "You gotta have a dream. You gotta work, you gotta learn to fail, you gotta surround yourself with greatness." And all of sudden they started staying in school and getting better grades.

MY DAUGHTER'S ACCOMPLISHMENTS AMAZE ME. I KNOW IT HASN'T BEEN EASY FOR HER. WALKING IN MY FOOTSTEPS HAS BEEN A DIFFICULT PATH FOR HER TO FOLLOW. *i'm so proud of kelly, i think she's one of our greatest athletes—she's a wonderful mother and a tremendous coach.*

I talked about the winning spirit, commitment, courage, adversities, failures, perseverance. I made a commitment to these kids that if they stayed in school and got good grades, I'd see that they had the opportunity for trade school or college. In 1984, I started on my own, using my own money, and in 1990 my first kid graduated from high school. He was a young Hispanic boy who was close to suicide at the time. His mother had overdosed and his sister had been shot. He was placed in our group and all he needed was a little TLC. He graduated, joined the army, went to Somalia and Haiti, is now out and married with two kids. We work with forty kids every other week. That's my legacy. It is one of the greatest gifts for me to know that I have purpose beyond myself.

From our only conversation before meeting, I discovered that Kelly McCormick is now a diving coach and a very proud mom. Pregnant with her third child, she would have preferred not to be seen in a bathing suit and hadn't done any diving in twelve years. I also learned that she has a love/hate relationship with her mother, Pat. What I learned after photographing Kelly is that her self-esteem overrides her self-consciousness, she still dives like a swan, and her relationship with her mom is like all of ours: multi-faceted, enduring, and very, very powerful.

Ironically, my mother did not influence my wanting to dive. But she probably planted the seed for me to be in the Olympics. In my junior high yearbook, I wrote, "I want to go to the 1976 Olympics in gymnastics." My mother used to arrange these huge water shows for charity at our house two or three weekends in a row, packing in hundreds of people. We'd have four sets of bleachers in our backyard. We had a built-in trampoline and a huge ten-foot-deep pool with a one-meter diving board. I had to do this routine with my mother to "Me and My Shadow," and I hated it because I was always the shadow. And the media always put me in her shadow. That's why, when we were at her office one time, it was kind of a joke when she introduced me as the wayward daughter. She's always doing that, so I piped up and said sarcastically, "Yeah, I'm following in your footsteps."

When I was younger I always had to do these promotional things with her. She would always endorse, "Pat McCormick, the four-time Olympic gold medalist." It was always such a big deal with her, even now. That's her identity. It's been really difficult for me to deal with that. My daughter, Alexandria, didn't know until recently that I dived in the Olympics or even that I dived at all. I don't have any diving stuff up at my house at all—I'm proud of it but I don't want to push it down her throat either.

i'm really obsessive-compulsive. i like to be the best at whatever i do—i think it's just part of my personality. i don't think that's something that you can breed into someone; either you're a fighter or you're not . . . and i am.

I think the best time my mother and I shared was just recently, when we went to get our tattoos. We had them done in Long Beach, California, at Bert Grime's World Famous Tattoo Studio, one of the oldest tattoo parlors in the United States. It was great because there was no press, no cameras, no hoopla, just me and my mom, and, of course, Rick the tattoo artist, who had been there forever and had seen many a night. When we first walked in, these guys just blew us off. They were a tough bunch: long hair, tattoos everywhere. After we got talking, said what we wanted, and told them the story behind the Olympic rings it was really cool. It turns out Rick's daughter had dived in high school and was currently a cheerleader on a national squad. We really had a great time with these guys. Of course, my mother made me go first to see if it hurt.

My parents had a bitter divorce. I think that is, in part, why I kept diving—to be closer to my father. Diving was his passion—he was my mother's coach, but he had an affair with another diver. But my dad was a great teacher. He was the U.S. judge in many Olympics, and we went on many, many trips together. I dived with my dad until I was about twenty-one.

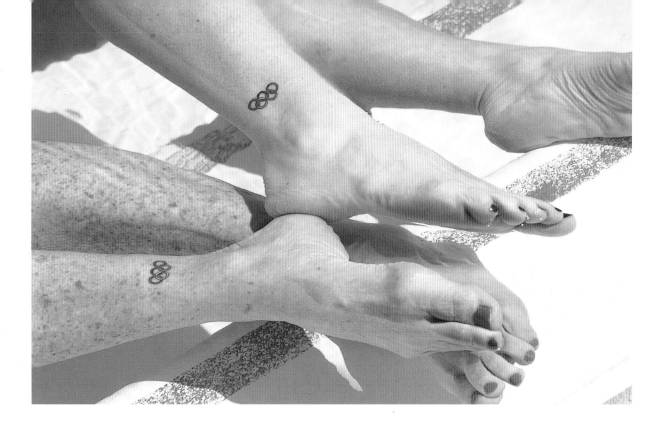

I don't know whether I became an athlete because of my genes or because I was really hyperactive as a child. We spent a lot of time outdoors growing up in California. I started gymnastics when I was eight. U.S. Olympian Cathy Rigby gave me private lessons and I was on the Long Beach Scats for seven or eight years. I became an elite gymnast but got out of it because if I asked them if I could go on vacation to ski, I'd come back and be dropped a class. That really pissed me off. So I quit gymnastics when I was fourteen and started playing around with diving. The next summer I was an alternate on an age-group national team. Someone got hurt and I got to compete on a U.S. team in Europe. There were boys and girls on this team, and although we got in trouble for drinking and being out late, we had a blast. That's what got me hooked.

Having gone to about three different high schools, I finally graduated from night school. My mom kicked me out of the house when I was seventeen, and I moved in with my boyfriend and his family. Then, I quit diving for awhile and tried work as a hostess. But I hated it and started diving again. Then, when I was nineteen, my buddy Lenny and I both won scholarships to the University of Miami. I fell in love with a guy and went back to California after about a semester. I thought it was love, but he ended up being very abusive.

I went to Long Beach State but fell in with the wrong crowd. I knew if I wanted to make it to the Olympic team I had to get my act together. I had talent coming out my ears, but because I was so wild nobody wanted to touch me. Then I met Vince Panzanno, the coach at Ohio State. He and I just hit it off right away, and he agreed to let me train with him. I arrived at Ohio State two weeks later. That is where I had all my successes as a diver and where I found my pseudofamily. I hardly ever came home after that. We were a group of about fifteen divers and called ourselves the "fun bunch." The problem was we were all really wild. And we were always doing stuff to Vince. One day we walked in—this was 1982–83, long before people even colored their hair—and we had all colored our hair bright pink. We didn't know at the time but the guy is color-blind so that didn't work out too well.

Vince often had to take off for out-of-town meets and would be gone the whole month, so we would have to train on our own. There was a lot of discipline there—it took a lot of hard work. I was very proud of that. The camaraderie was amazing; we were, after all, the fun bunch. We could stay up and party and then just kick everybody's butt. It wasn't a very good regimen, but I think that's why we kept doing it.

I remember the twenty-first birthday of one of my teammates. We had a big party and I fell asleep on someone's couch. When I woke up I had missed the bus to Nationals. I called my mom, who said, "Just get to the airport." So I flew to Pennsylvania. I got there about fifteen minutes into their workout. The coach said, "McCormick, optionals!" (Optionals are

it's a complex and confusing relationship that my mom and i have. i don't love her for her medals or her accomplishments, which is not to say i'm not proud of her. but i love her when she is just pat. funny, energetic, with a big heart. that's my mom.

your harder dives: you're twisting and somersaulting two-and-a-half times.) I was still a bit on the shaky side, but I redeemed myself and won my first national title.

My first Olympic trials were in 1980. I had a back injury. Nobody could diagnose it; when I got up in the morning I could barely breathe. I went to Cincinnati, where they did this thermal heat thing and found I had a dislocated rib, so they put me in traction for a week—this was all just a month before the Olympic trials. Back then, there were at least twelve

people that could have won the two places on the Olympic team. When I was in traction, some buddies of mine showed up with a bottle of tequila and other goodies and we partied in my hospital room. When I got out of the hospital I wanted to quit diving. I was so weak I couldn't make my dives. Vince came over to my house and said, "What are you gonna tell your kids some day? That you would have made it, that you could have made it?" He said this wasn't me, the fighter, trying to do it. So I hung in there and ended up going and I beat everybody by a hundred points or so. I didn't even have to do my last dive. Some of the other coaches had certain attitudes toward me. I was considered the black sheep of diving, the underdog. So it was always nice to think: "Don't get mad, get even."

I don't think I was a good role model. I had a lot of problems I had to work through. And I have. I was a good teammate. I never really considered myself on top, because you're only as good as your last meet. I have my own diving team now, with about forty kids. We take a boom box with us when we travel. We invent games. I want to teach them that you have to have fun. You've got to be imaginative. You can work your butt off and still have fun. I really believe that.

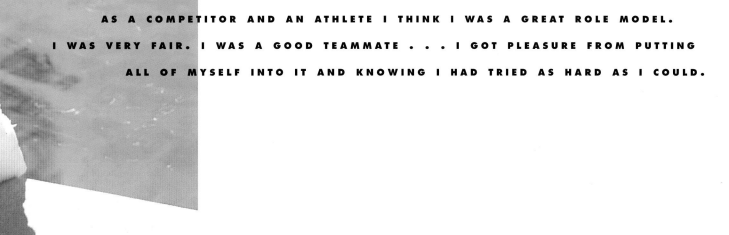

AS A COMPETITOR AND AN ATHLETE I THINK I WAS A GREAT ROLE MODEL. I WAS VERY FAIR. I WAS A GOOD TEAMMATE . . . I GOT PLEASURE FROM PUTTING ALL OF MYSELF INTO IT AND KNOWING I HAD TRIED AS HARD AS I COULD.

LUCIA
R I J K E R

w.i.b.f. european boxing champion, 1997—98
current u.s. record: 10—0

The Wildcard Gym was exactly what I had expected: hot, humid, and dimly lit, with spit buckets and gray walls. It has dozens of boxing posters on the walls of men, with one exception—a poster that portrays Lucia Rijker, or, as they call her, "Lady Ali." When Rijker sees me, she turns to shake my hand and I am shocked at how beautiful she is, an exotic version of Raquel Welch. Her agent senses my wonder at her unmarred face and proudly announces her undefeated boxing streak. Over ten matches in the U.S., most knock-outs in early rounds, preceded by a kickboxing record of 36—0, twenty-five of which were won by first-round knockouts. She skill-fully dances around the punching bag, telling me that she has just completed a course in self-empowerment, critiquing it all the while without missing a shot. Her mind is just as phenomenal as her body.

About a year ago, I fought this girl. At the weigh-in, I looked at her and thought she was a man. And everyone else was looking at her and saying, "It's a dude, man, it's a dude." She was very, very tough. My fear was talking. So I went to the ocean and chanted for about three hours and then I realized that a sword is useless in the hands of a cow-ard. It was time to prove that I'm a real champion. I went in there with a glow from all the chanting I did and knocked her out in the fifth round, through the ropes. After a fight, I normally jump into the arms of my trainer, but I had switched trainers. My new one is small and has kind of a problem with his ankle, and when I jumped on him he almost fell. So I lifted him up, and it was amazing. I lifted my trainer above my head.

My brother was an important influence in the beginning of my career and he still is my biggest fan. My parents basi-cally had nothing to say so I guess I just did what I wanted from day one. My father and I had a lot of unresolved issues—I needed an outlet for my emotions. I started competing when I was six years old. I started with judo and then began softball. I was a city champion and played nationally as a catcher. Then I started fencing and became the Dutch fencing champion. After that I started karate and went up to the full belt and then my brother inspired me to begin kickboxing when I was fourteen years old. I won my first world title when I was sixteen. After that, I took four more world titles.

— 31 —

I THINK I CAN MAKE A

DIFFERENCE BY SHARING

WITH PEOPLE HOW I

GOT WHERE I AM—

THROUGH FOCUS, DISCI-

PLINE AND DEDICATION

i've found incredible inner strength through chanting and meditation.
i've grown so much—i've learned about myself and my relationships, i've learned to
deal with people and treat others well.

lucia and trainer freddy roach, wildcard gym, 1998

I've always felt very much at home in the gym where I worked out, and whatever I did, I gave 200 percent. I wanted to be the best. Where that came from I have no idea. I just wanted to master things that I did and this was one of them. I started boxing because it was a challenge. It was similar to kickboxing yet different. It's like switching from basketball to volleyball. After those eleven years of kickboxing, I moved to the U.S. and picked up boxing. I became the European champion and world champion, and that was it.

I went to a training camp once with seven guys from the inner city— seven really tough boxers. We lived in one house, and I had to lock my door. It was awful. I mean, I had seven brothers all of a sudden. But it was interesting to see where a real boxer comes from, what kind of lifestyle he leads. It seemed like a miracle that I survived. I remember I won my next fight with a third-round knockout, but boy was I happy to get out of that place. It felt like I was in prison.

To be one of the best in my sport gives me a powerful feeling of acceptance, appreciation, and accomplishment. Especially when you are good at a sport that men dominate. Being a woman on top gives you self-confidence and a sense of empowerment, which many women don't have naturally. And to be appreciated and acknowledged in a male-dominant sport is for me a big accomplishment and a challenge at the same time. You know you work hard, you get hit just like guys; the only difference is we fight two-minute rounds. Although when it comes down to money we get paid nothing compared to the guys.

I once met Muhammad Ali, a man that I so admire for everything that he did for humanity and how he paid with his health. He was full of light and enthusiasm and joy and wisdom—just a great, great man. I was honored to meet him and I asked him to look at my last fight, and he did. He said he was very impressed. He is my role model. That's what I would like to be—a role model, to make a difference in other people's lives. And I'm sure I will. For me, a role model is about just being the best that I can be and stretching myself and challenging myself as a woman in a man's sport, without trying to be a man in a man's sport.

every day i struggle with my femininity. boxing is such a boy's club—i'm constantly on guard. it's taken a lot of work, but i finally feel that what makes me a woman is what gives me my power.

ROCHELLE

BALLARD

the number-two ranked female surfer in the u.s.
the world's premier barrel-riding woman

Rochelle Ballard picks me up at the airport. With her are two other surfers, Serena and Megan. Rochelle is the big sister—the only
one old enough to drive the rental car. The girls have been on tour and are dying to go to the mall. Amidst a whirl of shoes, shirts , bras,
makeup, and giggles, Serena reminds everyone that they could be catching some waves instead. A frenzy of action occurs—with wet
suits, ankle straps, and board bags flying, we're suddenly racing to the beach with three surfboards precariously perched on top of the
car. Before I can so much as blink, the girls have already plunged into the ice-cold water on their way to catch the perfect wave.

I started surfing when I was twelve years old. My parents moved to the island of Kauai when I was a baby. It was
the seventies; my dad surfed and they just wanted to hang out and play. It was an unpopulated island—a really beautiful place with a lot of good waves. I learned to swim even before I learned to walk, and my dad got me into surfing; I always watched him. I loved everything about the ocean—swimming, diving, playing on the beach. We lived
down the street from surfing legend and mentor Margo Oberg. She was a top professional surfer for more than three
decades. I really admired her "big wave" surfing. She received so much respect for what she did. She took me out
surfing quite a bit one year, spent time with me, gave me pointers, and encouraged me to brave larger waves. I developed a love for surfing, a love that is almost impossible to express. There's an energy in the water that gives you
every kind of feeling: peace, excitement, fear, a huge adrenaline rush, discouragement, frustration. The nature of
surfing is such that you can't control the waves. You have to flow with them and find the rhythm of the ocean in
order to work with it and experience what the ocean has to offer. Surfing is an art—we draw a new line on each wave
we ride. It's also a science. You need to study the patterns of the ocean. And it's an ongoing lesson, because every
few years, the tides completely change.

I have a lot of physical energy and coordination and I'm a competitive person. My competitiveness was enhanced
by the neighborhood guys I surfed with. I did everything with them: dirt biking, jumping ramps, and skateboarding.
When we were surfing, they used reverse psychology. On big wave days, they would say, "You can't surf out
there!" I always proved them wrong. I started doing contests locally and had fun with it and did well. I carried it on
to state competitions, and then into the nationals, and to the world amateur titles. Thereafter came pro-surfing, what's
known as the ASP, or Association of Surfing Professionals. You have to qualify to get into the World Championship
Tour. I'm part of the top eight—which is actually now the top eleven. It's an elite group of female surfers striving
to be the best and become world champions, which is my ultimate goal.

I feel like I have accomplished as much as I can at the moment. I've won quite a few contests, and I've influenced women's surfing in ways that I've always wanted to: inspiring young girls to get out in the water and just express themselves and enjoy what God has given us. I'm a Christian and I love the Lord with all my heart. I think that brings me a peace that nothing else can compare to. I'm thankful for what I've been given and the opportunity to be able to compete and to surf in the water.

Surfers are given a gift from God: having waves and being able to ride them. We have different surfer foundations that take care of the ocean. They play a great role in keeping the ocean clean and protecting the environment, and also in setting up different wave venues. I think that God has put us here to preserve the waves; I'm very spiritual about it.

Then there's the competitive side of it. You get out there and you try to compete for twenty-five minutes in a heat and hope that everything comes together for you. It involves a lot of skill tactics, mind preparation, getting into a flow and rhythm with the ocean, and having wave knowledge. It takes years and years to build up wave knowledge—where to sit, where the best wave is coming in, what waves are going to be good, what waves are going to be bad—and you keep learning as you go along. There's quite a bit of luck involved in surfing because you're dealing with elements of nature. The other surfer can catch the best wave while you don't get anything, even though you know exactly where you're sitting and exactly what's going on. It's just the nature of the beast. You could see the best wave come through and unfortunately, somebody else is riding it. And sometimes you surf to your potential and catch the best waves and still the other person just out-surfs you. That's the way it is.

THE SKY'S THE LIMIT. I'M STILL STRIVING, REACHING UP TO THE CLOUDS, TAKING IT AS FAR AS I CAN, AND JUST ENJOYING EVERY SINGLE MINUTE ALONG THE WAY.

BEING TRULY SUCCESSFUL MEANS

HAVING THE TIME AND

FREEDOM TO BE ABLE TO ENJOY

THE COMPANY OF THE PEOPLE

YOU CARE ABOUT.

we travel around the world together as a group of forty-four guys and eleven women. we're each others' family. my father is often my biggest fan on tour.

THIS ISN'T AN ABSTRACT

PHILOSOPHY FOR ME—I'VE

BEEN DULY BLESSED

IN THAT MY BEST FRIENDS ARE

PART OF MY JOB.

When I first started I remember being out in the water and competing and the guys would say, "Oh, you're good for a girl." I used to get super bummed out. I thought, "I just want to be good, I want to be like the guys." Then I finally got to a point where I thought, "You know what, forget that. I'm proud to be a woman and I love being an athlete and physically fit. This is the way I am, and it feels good and it's healthy and it makes me happy." I'm proud to be a female athlete and to have female role models—other female athletes as my mentors—rather than just the men. We finally have the freedom to be who we are instead of trying to be like the men. We just get out there and do it. It's a great feeling.

Surfing is a lifestyle. Being a part of the ocean, having the freedom to play on the beach in the sun, wearing bathing suits, being with your friends—all that good stuff gets carried through in the sport of surfing. And the life of a pro-surfer is full of adventure and excitement. The best thing about traveling on a circuit is that you experience different cultures. In South Africa, I surfed the most beautiful wave—one of the best waves in the world. There was a lot of wildlife out there—sharks, whales, seals, and dolphins. A school of dolphins would come through and ride the waves. They have priority out there. It's a beautiful thing to see—the sky is golden and lit up and there's a fresh smell. The wind blows the top off the crest of the wave and feathers it offshore. I remember thinking, "This is what it is to be a surfer."

F E R N A N D E Z

olympic gold medalist, fast-pitch softball, 1996

four-time n.c.a.a. all-american

n.c.a.a. woman of the year, 1993

Lisa Fernandez's father was a semi-pro baseball player in Cuba before coming to the States. Her mother was born in Puerto Rico and grew up playing stickball in the streets of New York. Mr. Fernandez answers the door in full workout attire accompanied by his two-year-old granddaughter (Lisa's niece) in her tiny sweats and sneakers. While waiting for Lisa to arrive, he demonstrates the little girl's skill at "T" ball in front of a Lisa Fernandez shrine—medals, trophies, even a framed high school jersey. Lisa's mom proudly volunteers some newspaper clippings about Lisa for my research. Playing ball is definitely a Fernandez family affair.

My parents used to play in coed slow-pitch leagues. My sister played also. So I guess I've always been around the sport. I got my first picture in the paper with a paddle-tennis paddle taking a swing at the ball—the caption read, "Like your mom says, you have to keep your eye on the ball." And there I was taking a swing with my eyes closed. I guess that was my start in softball as a hitter.

I was very competitive from the start. I first played softball at a sports clinic for kids too young to join leagues. When I was about seven, a man named Al Mendoza asked me to try out for his softball team. So I practiced with my mom in the backyard, slow-pitching the ball into a bucket. At the tryout, Mr. Mendoza asked me to pitch. But when I got on the rubber and lobbed the ball, I heard him say from the outfield, "Hey! what are you doing? This is fast-pitch. Throw the ball as hard and as straight across the plate as you can for a strike." I gave it a whirl—and got the starting job. Our team was called the Dirty Dozen, a "little miss" team out of Long Beach, California. It was the beginning of my fast-pitch career.

I'll never forget our first game. I was so excited that I got ready at 7 a.m. for a noon game. When I got on the mound, I saw the catcher with all of this gear and a big burly umpire with a mask on—I realized it was a lot different than slow-pitch. The first three pitches I threw were balls and then the next pitch hit the girl right in the head. By the end of the game, we had lost 25–0, and I had walked about twenty batters and hit about twenty. I walked off the field feeling pretty down. Then my mom said, "At least you have a choice. You can go on and try and get better or you can stay as you are." I made the decision at that time to go on and be the best that I could be.

I knew I wasn't going to improve overnight but I worked at getting better step-by-step. My mom used to challenge me by seeing how many times I could hit her gloved target. At first it was one out of ten and two days later it was two out of ten and five days later it was four out of ten. And then I was hitting my spots nine out of ten times. Even though my team lost, it was a victory—because from that I saw how much I was able to improve and what it meant to go one step at a time.

MY DAD, DESPITE HIS FRIENDS' HECKLING, WAS ALWAYS SUPPORTIVE. WHEN I WON THE GOLD MEDAL, HE WORE IT AROUND HIS NECK TO SHOW HIS FRIENDS. HE TOLD THEM, "THIS IS WHAT MY DAUGHTER DOES."

My mother was my first coach, first catcher, and first pitcher. My dad worked nights, so we saw very little of him. But we made up for lost time on the weekends when he took me to as many games as possible—men's and women's—to watch and learn about fast-pitch softball. We would study, experiment with, and try to emulate different techniques until I found one that worked for me.

In Hispanic culture, girls are not usually encouraged to be athletic. My dad's support was a big step in my development. He gets heckled a bit by his friends, but his pride shines through. When I first signed with Florida Southern I came out with a poster, and my dad took it to his friends beaming. Shortly after came a signed bat and he said, "This is what my daughter does!" When I won the Olympic gold medal my dad wore it around his neck for days—he wanted everyone to know. It would have been impossible without his support.

When I was twelve I went to see a very well-known pitching coach. We went into his office and he looked at my arms, asking me to straighten them. I have a little dip in my elbow that doesn't allow me to straighten my arm fully, and he said, "I don't think you'll pitch past the age of sixteen. Your arms aren't long enough and you don't have the right build." And I said, "What do I have to do?" and he answered, "You can come to me, we'll try to hook you up to a few machines—maybe we can change your style, but there is no guarantee." After we left his office I started to cry, thinking, "How could my career be over even before it had begun?" I was destroyed. My mom turned around and yelled at me: "Stop crying! If you let someone else tell you what you can and can't do you're never going to make it." That really influenced me.

People don't realize just how fast the ball is thrown in our sport. From forty-three feet away, a woman pitcher can throw a ball that is clocked at 67 miles per hour. The ball reaches the plate in .39 seconds. In comparison, Nolan Ryan throws from sixty-six feet, six inches away and is clocked at 101 miles per hour and the ball reaches the plate in .40 seconds. So a women fast-ball pitcher throws the ball faster in terms of reaction time than a Nolan Ryan fast ball. When you're at bat and you come through with a key base hit, it's not for yourself but for the team; there is no other feeling like it. You feel like you are invincible. When you are a pitcher, the bases are loaded, and you're facing the number-four hitter in the lineup, what are you going to do? What are you going to throw? What strategy have you developed in analyzing her hitting style to be able to get her out? What changes are you going to make? Different changes, different adjustments. There's nothing better than coming through for the team.

Six years ago there wasn't one endorsement spot available for women who played fast-pitch softball. Now we have many. I was the first to have a signature bat from Louisville Slugger. I helped them design fast-pitch equipment. Before, we had to use gear that was designed for men who hit slow-pitch. We were expected to hit a ball coming at us faster than you can imagine with equipment that wasn't suited for the sport. Other companies got involved and now girls can wear equipment that is suited for them. Shoe companies are coming up with designs for a cleat made for fast-

FOR MEN IT HAS ALWAYS BEEN OKAY TO SWEAR, CUSS, BE TICKED OFF, SHOW THEIR AGGRESSION; BUT IF YOU'RE A WOMAN, YOU'RE NOT EVEN SUPPOSED TO SWEAT . . . BUT I THINK THE IMAGE IS CHANGING. IT IS SLOWLY BECOMING ACCEPTABLE FOR A WOMAN TO SWEAT, WORK, FIGHT, AND SHOW TEARS, BUT STILL PLAY WITH THE GUTS AND RESOLVE OF A MAN.

pitch softball. None of this would be possible without the pioneers who came before us: Nancy Hogshead in swimming, Donna de Varona in swimming, Martina Navratilova in tennis, Jill St. James in auto racing, Jackie Joyner-Kersee in track. When I step on the field it's those pioneers who I represent, as well as female athletes like Billie Jean King and Donna Lopiano, who developed the Women's Sports Foundation, which brings together the top women in sports. Women are coming together to fight for what they believe in.

Sports have taught me how to set goals, achieve dreams, and perform under pressure. I have learned how to be a team player, how to work for something, how to fail and succeed. I think sports are important for kids because they teach those life skills. And although we have many positive influences around us, only we can control our own destinies. The only limitations are those you put on yourself.

my mother didn't have the opportunities that i had in

organized sports, but she was committed to my success.

now, my niece is the future. as a female athlete, i know the

roadblocks that lie ahead for her. i will try to eliminate those

by always conducting myself with dignity and pride—i put my best

foot forward to set an example for her and pave the road

for all the women who will come along after me.

I learned a valuable lesson when I was a senior at UCLA. It was at the championship—the last day I would wear a Bruin uniform. We were playing the University of Arizona and I was on the mound. The first batter hit the ball short and got on first base. The second batter sacrificed her to second. One out, two strikes on the hitter, and I threw a pitch and the girl hit it up the middle. She got a base hit and my center fielder threw it home, a run scored; Arizona was up 1–0 in the top of the first inning. Second, third, fourth, fifth, sixth, and seventh innings go by and we didn't score and lost 1–0. I walked off that field and thought I had nothing to cry about—I gave everything I had and so did the team. At an interview after the game a reporter raised his hand and said: "Lisa, you have won numerous awards in your career as a collegiate athlete, numerous All-American awards, Honda awards, a lot of accolades, how does it feel to go out as a loser?" It wasn't until I heard this that tears

"IF I HAD TO DECIDE WHAT HAS TOUCHED ME MOST THROUGHOUT MY ATHLETIC EXPERIENCE, IT WOULD HAVE TO BE THE TALENTED PEOPLE THAT SURROUNDED ME. *you work with multitudes of personalities and skill levels. it's incredibly gratifying to help mold them and, in turn, have them mold me."*

– sharon baccus

actually came to my eyes. It was as though my whole entire being was changed by one performance. I realized that we can't control whether we win or lose, but we can control ourselves—what we sacrifice, our work ethic, and how much we dedicate. My motto in life and sport is: "be the best that I can be at whatever level that is." That's all I can ask of myself. When that desire fades, then I will know that it's time for me to retire.

My coach at UCLA, Sharon Baccus, has been one of my biggest inspirations. She was a player herself in the seventies at UCLA. She always said, "In this society, there are a lot of ways opportunities are limited because of gender. Never forget to see people as people and take advantage of every opportunity that you have to play. Be the kind of person who takes the negative and turns it into a positive. Sports help us to prepare to become members of a collective team. Things have changed dramatically in sports and business. People are now recruited for experience and knowledge rather than their sex. The opportunities are there, and as women, we must take advantage of them."

K R O N E

history's most celebrated female jockey,
with more than 3,300 trips to the winner's circle

winner, belmont stakes, 1993

Julie Krone is small. It's hard to imagine her at four feet, ten-and-a-half inches tall and a hundred pounds atop a two-thousand-pound animal going over forty miles per hour. But as one of the legendary jockeys of the century, Julie has a riding style with an element of mystery that goes beyond the physical. In fact, it's been said that Julie Krone's relationship with horses is almost spiritual. Unfortunately, it's a rainy day in Miami when I photograph Julie, and the jockeys vote to stop riding for the day. My chance for an action shot that day is foiled. Exhausted and covered in mud, Julie offers to show me how it's done on the wooden training horse. With little enthusiasm I watch her mount the lifeless creature. She closes her eyes and begins to whisper and chirp to egg him on faster. Her intensity transcends the situation. She's simply magical.

When I was a child in Eau Claire, Michigan, I used to put on this little snowsuit and watch my mother play with our horse. He would wait for her to crunch the snow together in her hand and then he would take off running before she threw the snowball at him. Then he would come back and they would do it again. When he was finished he would stand and blow steam out of his nose and my mother would pet his head. My mom has always had a special way with horses, and fortunately, some of her abilities to communicate with horses rubbed off on me a little bit.

As a child, if I saw somebody do something, I would say, "I can do that." I was very determined and tried really hard and hustled a lot. No matter what I did—even if it was Wiffleball in the backyard—if it was athletic, I took it very seriously. I really liked to win. I decided to become a jockey mainly because of Stevie Cauthen's influence. After watching him win the Triple Crown in 1978, I would imitate him by sitting on a trunk with my baseball hat on backwards holding a fly swatter, pretending I was riding. Then I said, "Mom, I want to be a jockey," and she and I went to Kentucky together. That trip was the turning point in my life. We started going to the library and reading about racehorses and the racetrack and what would be expected. I was sixteen years old when we decided that I would quit high school and work at the track as a groom and exercise girl. After a grueling year, my lucky break came when I began to race quarter horses and win. In 1980, I left home for good to pursue my dream at Tampa Bay Downs. The rest is history. That's some visioning, you know, from childhood to almost adulthood. I wanted to win the Belmont like Steve Cauthen. I always dreamed of that happening and it did.

It's a pretty special feeling to ride without hitting the horse with the whip. The horse reaches into its heart and delivers every single bit of what it's capable of. You just motion your hands and the horse follows you, almost as if it reads your mind, and everything goes right. Winning the Belmont in 1993 was one of those days. I remember it like it was yesterday. After I got a leg-up, I patted Colonial Affair on the neck and said, "Let's go make history, Buddy." He stood beautifully in the gate. We broke fast, and he was immediately in my hands—not pulling too hard, but perfectly balanced. Colonial Affair was "right on" that day. I had been riding him since he was two years old. He indicated to me that all I needed to do was just let him know when I wanted to go faster. I waited, conserving his energy for the backstretch. There were nine horses ahead of us when we made our move. Even as I watched the jockeys push their horses to the limit, I knew we were going to win. I chirped to him and threw my reins and he sprouted wings. When we crossed the wire my mind went blank. All I could hear was a tiny voice saying, "We won the Belmont, we *won* the Belmont." I had become the first female jockey in the 125-year history to cross the finish line first. Life isn't made up of such incredibly high moments, but they sure do feel good.

Being successful feels a little bit different now than it did when I was a younger athlete. It's typical for someone to think, "Oh, you're young, you're rude, or maybe you're careless with money." I was a little bit of a highfalutin kid, maybe too impressed by big paychecks and other things. Now I have a more down-to-earth attitude, and I really appreciate things. I've been at the bottom, I've been at the top, I've been in between. Now I maintain my

happiness and inner strength whether I win or I lose. My frame of mind isn't completely gauged by how I performed that day at the races. I used to beat myself up until I went out and proved myself again. I didn't have very much self-confidence. I'm a more mature person now— stronger, more centered, and with different things on my mind.

When people ask, "How does it feel to be a girl jockey?" I can't say, "Let's see, when I was a boy jockey it felt like that, and now that I'm a girl jockey it feels like this." Everyone in sports has times when something's held against them because of who they are, what color they are or their gender. I recently saw a documentary about Tiger Woods. When he was playing golf as a young boy, he was thrown out of a tournament because he tossed his club on the ground. And he said to his mother: "But mom, the white kids do it all the time, they don't get thrown out." His mom said, cut and dry: "Tiger, you're not those guys, only worry about what you do." That's the approach I take when I feel like I've been treated unfairly. I got a big kick out of an article written by a guy who didn't care much for girl jockeys. He watched racing all year and then finally had to fess up to it, that I was just as good, if not better, than some of the male jockeys. The top of the article read, "TOO DAMN BAD SHE'S A GIRL." It's kind of funny—sooner or later, people who want to see are going to open up their hearts and their eyes, and they're going to notice that a lot of incredible things can happen when people are given chances.

THERE'S COMPETITIVENESS—BUT WE SUPPORT EACH OTHER. IT'S AN INCREDIBLE THING, HOW FEMALE ATHLETES HANDLE SUCH POWERFUL, CONFLICTING EMOTIONS. *we're aggressive, but when the race is over we're comforting and caring to each other.*

Some of the girl jockeys are as close to me as sisters. There is a unique intensity or emotion that girls bring to things. It's fun to joke around in the girls' jock room and there might be a little bit of competitiveness and some aggressive verbal volley. But there is also a mutual admiration. It's interesting to see girls go out there and ride, be really aggressive and risk their lives—and then they come back and are supportive of one another.

I think a lot about the impression I might make on young fans. It means a great deal to me that they take away the impression that I am a good sport, even if I lose. I think I've set a good example. Especially since I was really successful and then had some very bad spills and went through a traumatic time when the quality of my riding diminished. In August 1993, I had a near-fatal accident. A twelve-hundred-pound horse hit me directly above my heart and my ankle was pulverized. It wasn't my first fall or broken bone but—God willing—it will be my worst. I don't remember falling. There was a flash of sound and color jumbled together in a single moment, then there was nothing—just dry turf under my back and a lot of pain.

My first thought was: "It's all spoiled." I even had a date planned when I was going to win my three-thousandth race, but it seemed like that would never happen. These thoughts soon faded to feelings of pain. If someone had held a gun to my head and offered to shoot, I would have considered the offer. It was a long, slow road to recovery.

During that period I felt very depressed and sad, riding with trepidation and constantly second-guessing myself. Slowly but surely, I worked my way out of it. It feels good to have broken through those barriers. I didn't just ride on the shirttails of success. I had to show grit and determination, to experience pain and some pretty terrible times, and then come back for more. So maybe that leaves an impression with girls and women in sports. Scars are a bit like jewelry. And I wear plenty of jewelry now.

there's a marvelous side to all horses—but you have to earn their trust to find it. once you do, they'll always respect and care for you. there's nothing as good for the inside of a person as the outside of a horse.

G I O V E

world cup champion,
downhill mountain bike racing, 1996 and 1997

Missy Giove's dad recounted a story about Missy's fearless personality as a child. "We lived in Vermont, and she used to go out for hours on her bike with the boys. Missy was the leader. One night there was a terrible snowstorm. The kids had gone out that afternoon and didn't return. My wife and I were in a panic. The next morning, in walks Missy, tattered but triumphant, followed by two boys looking white as ghosts:'Dad, we were socked in, so I built a shelter and we sat it out, it was incredible!'" Not only is she tough, Missy is also a combination of cool—with her shock of black hair and nose ring—and mystical. She just built a Mongolian yurt for meditating in her backyard and always carries her dead dog's ashes during a race. She also wears a dead piranha (a deceased pet) around her neck, but today it's at the taxidermist, something about damage in customs . . .

Some people look at me like I have three heads. I am often misunderstood because I present myself differently. I look different from the next person, and I might act different than the average woman, but I am just expressing myself. I do what I want—but never at the expense of others. What you put out into the world comes back to you three times over. There's a difference between crazy and dumb.

It's funny because people think I'm some madwoman on a bike—but that's what the press represents to the public. The madwoman is part of me. There are times on my bike when I'll just let it all rage and just hang out and be crazy because I have to, but there's a method to my madness.

Before I start a run, I sit on my bike up on the mountain and relax. I get confident and comfortable with myself and with the course, and I try to become one with nature. If you don't have respect for the land it's going to eat you up. I research everything to prepare for a race—every aspect of a course, including wind patterns. But your mind is the number-one element of success—you have to be able to concentrate and focus. I do my best when I'm totally dialed in. If you're thinking about what you're having for dinner, you're going to have a bad run.

The keys for me are mental training techniques and diligently following a program. You have to create a familiar environment that is as consistent as possible: same wake-up time, same breakfast, same warm-up ritual, same bike preparation, same mental preparation, some song to get you pumped. I practice visualization several hours a day—two hours before bed, one hour in the morning before practice. I do some candle magic and hug a tree on the course. The day before a competition I race to get out all the tension and be clean in my head and heart. I also talk to my friends and family and tell them I love them—just in case I don't get another chance to. Then I'm ready to roll—to walk the path of the peaceful warrior with only one thing on my mind: to win.

MY FIRST TIME ON A MOUNTAIN BIKE, I CRASHE

FORTY MILES AN HOUR DOWN A SKI SLOPE WHEN I HIT A WATER BAR. I DID A NO

NEXT WATER BAR, FLIPPED, AND LANDED FORTY YARDS DOWN THE HILL. I GOT UP, GOT

A MAN NAMED CHARLIE LITSKY SAW THIS AND SAID, "I'VE NEVER SEEN A WOMA

EALLY HARD. I WAS GOING
HEELIE ALL THE WAY TO THE
Y BIKE AND DID IT AGAIN.
O THAT! YOU'RE PSYCHOTIC."

Motivation is the key to success in whatever you are doing in life. It comes a lot easier when you are doing something that you love or are working toward something that you have a passion for. I love my sport and have put myself in contention to be on top of the competition for six years; obviously I'm not going to aim for anything lower. My goal is to have a good time and a hot run. And I'm not afraid of disappointment—it only makes me work harder.

I thrive on fear. I like to see how much I can push myself to the border. Before I start an important race, I say to myself, "You're going to have to ride really fast and really scare yourself to win." When I'm God-awful close to a tree or the edge of a cliff, I try to get through it by believing in myself and saying, "I can pull this off," rather than hitting the brake. Sometimes when you hang it all out, you crash. If I don't make it, I learn from my mistake. I guess I need to learn that I don't need to go as fast as I can all the time. The odds are going to be against you; sooner or later, something is going to happen. And I plan to be bike racing for a long time—until I'm no longer having fun.

I don't usually get hurt—maybe it's because I'm not afraid. But when I do crash, my reaction is usually, "I just survived! I didn't believe I was going to live and I survived!" It makes me feel immortal, as though I could jump off a plane and live. And I accept the pain as a part of the sport: the injuries, the hunger, the cold, pushing yourself to the threshold day in and day out, the agony of defeat, the sorrow of starting all over again, the fear of failure and success. For me the whole thing is a big journey. I feel like an artist: Every course I go to, I'm creating a new masterpiece.

I got into mountain racing because my friends practically made me do it. I had learned how to handle a bike when I delivered Chinese food on the Upper East Side of New York. But my first time on a mountain bike was at a race at Mount Snow in Vermont and I won. I also crashed really, really hard. I was going about forty miles an hour

i try to combine the qualities of masculine and feminine.
if i can be aggressive and cooperative, i can do really well.

down this ski slope—because I had no concept of what you can and can't do on a mountain bike—when I hit a water bar. I did a nose wheelie all the way to the next water bar, flipped, and landed about forty yards down the hill. I got up with grass sticking out of my helmet, got back on my bike, and did the same thing again. A man named Charlie Litsky saw this and said, "I've never seen a woman do that. You're psychotic." So he got a local bike shop to lend me a bike and pay for my entry fees.

MOTIVATION IS THE KEY TO SUCCESS IN WHATEVER YOU'RE DOING IN LIFE. IT COMES A LOT EASIER WHEN YOU'RE DOING SOMETHING YOU LOVE AND HAVE A PASSION FOR. *my goal is to have a good time and a hot run. and i'm not afraid of disappointment—it only makes me work harder.*

A lot of people make judgments about me that aren't based on who I am, but what they see or read. I get misinterpreted a lot, and people maybe are intimidated by me because they don't understand me. But there are people who take the time to know me and who I am, and what I stand for. They know that I'm open, honest, and upfront, and I don't try to become anybody I'm not. And I need my friends with me now. It's always more meaningful and wonderful when you can share your life and goals with others. Great friends and family are key. Love is the key for me.

I know I have things to work on, like my temper. My nature is hyper in general. I'm hyper just walking down the street, so if something happens, I'm going to react to it. I'm a full-blooded Sicilian woman. My father is my best friend, but he still yells at me—and I yell back. There's a lot of passion and emotion. When I was growing up in Manhattan, I was kicked out of several schools, because I've always questioned authority. I was both well-liked, because I was creative and I was my own person, and disliked, because teachers didn't like me questioning them. They didn't understand that I just wanted to further my knowledge. But my temper isn't directed so much toward other people as toward myself. I don't have much tolerance for my incompetence, and I've been giving away my power, not directing my energy toward cycling. But I've tried to get a hold of that. I think I'm doing a good job. I've learned the hard way that people will listen to you a lot more if you use sugar instead of vinegar.

Part of my purpose in setting high standards for myself is to establish a speed and technique that will challenge other women to rise above me. And I don't want to be just another world champion. I want to make a contribution to the sport. I started a foundation for women in mountain biking called the Amazon Foundation. It's open to everyone but aimed toward younger, non-white women who don't necessarily have the opportunity to ride bikes. One of the saddest things in this world is wasted talent. People should learn to not be afraid of success or failure because both will make you grow. I know that men and women will never be the same in terms of racing ability—gravity and physical strength benefit men. The gap between us will close only so far as we dare push our personal limits as women.

THOMPSON

Jenny arrives from the airport with a newly pierced nose now adorned with a delicate diamond. Her agent is nervous. "Has your mother seen that yet?" I pull out a temporary fish tattoo for Jenny to wear for a photo—she loves it. She is daring, confident, glamourous, and very determined. Tied with Bonnie Blair for the most Olympic gold medals won by an American woman, Thompson also holds more national championship titles than any other active swimmer. But she's not content to rest on her laurels. With the 2000 games ahead, Jenny's training schedule is rigorous enough. Yet somehow she will manage to fulfill her dream of completing medical school.

I'll never forget going to the Junior Nationals at the age of eight. That trip changed my life. It was a hot August day and because we couldn't afford to fly, my coach, his wife, my brother, and I drove from New Hampshire to Alabama in my coach's rusty old Datsun with no air conditioning. I placed sixth in the competition, even with a broken tailbone caused by sitting for so long on the old seat belt clasp in the car. That was the beginning of my competing well despite adversity.

To me, swimming is like brushing my teeth. I feel gross when I don't get to swim every day. Being a Pisces, I'm naturally drawn to the water. I was a water baby, swimming underwater at the age of six months, and by the time I turned seven, I was competing. When I was eight, I began serious training with Mike Perato at Sea Coast Swimming Association in New Hampshire, where I qualified for the Junior Nationals. My brother, who is several years older than me, qualified as well. We weren't just the only two people on our team to qualify, we were also the first from our club to go to the Nationals. We moved from Massachusetts to New Hampshire when I was twelve, so I could swim at a better facility. My parents are divorced, and my mother taught me and my three brothers to be independent. I learned to get myself to swim practice at a very young age.

Swimming helped me get a scholarship to Stanford University. Before Title IX, none of this would have happened. Before Title IX, there was no reason to swim beyond high school. Because of the scholarships, there are many older female swimmers still competing. Now we can become professionals and make a living. I have great endorsements from Speedo and others and I have been treated with respect. I get so many perks that sometimes I feel guilty, because I don't need all the freebies that come along with being a celebrity, and there are so many needy people out there. I guess that's just the way this world works, but I am trying to give back and help others to equal what I have received, which has been a lot.

IF IT'S POSSIBLE—I CAN DO IT
THAT'S THE ONE IDEAL THAT
MOST INFLUENCES AND SHAPES MY
PLANS FOR THE FUTURE. I KNOW EVENTUALL
I WANT TO SEE THE SPORT PROGRESS, BUT AS LONG AS I'M ABLE, I'

Sometimes you get caught up in winning instead of enjoying the competition. In 1992 I won a silver medal in the Olympics and was disappointed. I was going for gold. In 1994 I wanted to come back and have a really great World Championships. I was at the top of my game, swimming really well, and I thought I could break a few records. Then in May, just a few weeks before the games, I broke my arm and had to undergo surgery. But all I could think about was winning. One day I got caught by my coach working out in the gym with stitches—an absolute no-no. I was jeopardizing my future health for the immediate desire to win. I had to step back and reevaluate my priorities and decided to just compete for the love of swimming. It was ironic that that was the year the Chinese team broke all the records and the rules by using steroids.

ETTER SWIMMERS WILL SURPASS MY ACCOMPLISHMENTS.
IGHT TOOTH AND NAIL TO BE THE BEST.

Swimming has always been accepted as a sport for women, but sometimes I feel unattractive because I don't look feminine enough. I once dated a guy who said he liked me, but my arms freaked him out. I was traumatized. Are my arms too big, too ugly? Then I thought, "My arms are what make me swim so fast and they're part of who I am." The body issue is one of the last hurdles for women. Being a strong woman and an athlete isn't entirely acceptable in society. I notice that in men's sports there are always cameras showing an athlete's wife or

I'M BECOMING COMFORTABLE WITH WHO I AM AND THE WAY I LOOK. I LIKE MY MUSCLES NOW. I LOOK THIS WAY FOR A REASON; MY BODY HAS A PURPOSE— IT HELPS ME ACHIEVE MY GOALS. *female athletes are strong but that's what makes us beautiful.*

significant other. In women's sports they don't even ask about your boyfriend. It's as if they assume that since female athletes are strong, they must be asexual. We are strong, but that's what makes us beautiful.

M U L L I N S

paralympic world record holder, 100 meter and long jump
national record holder, 200 meter

Aimee Mullins was born without fibula bones in her shins. Her parents had to make the painful decision to amputate rather than see Aimee spend the rest of her life in a wheelchair. Now an elite athlete, she enters the room tall, thin, beautiful, and dressed in black with high leather boots. Aimee already looks like a model as she sits down with the makeup artist. She is incredibly outspoken and articulate about her cause as a handicapped athlete. My sister and I watched in awe as she removed her now famous and extremely realistic silicone leg for inspection. Her candor was inspiring. We joked about how much better her legs looked than our own. Suddenly, my sister began to sob: "I'll never complain about anything again. You've given me so much hope—I feel so ashamed of myself for complaining about my miniscule problems." Now everyone is crying and nodding in agreement. In true Aimee Mullins style, she took my sister's hand and said, "I'm just like you—no better, no worse. We all have our crosses to bear. We're all fighting for happiness and inner peace. That's what counts." I don't think anyone is ever quite the same after meeting Aimee.

As a child, I was never treated differently because I'm an amputee. That's the only way I can explain why I have always been so competitive. We had races running from our back porch to the end of the yard, and I never got any slack—it was just expected that I would compete like the others. I think it's the best way to raise somebody with a disability because I didn't grow up with any excuses. So not only did I participate, I strove to excel. My parents supported me in anything I wanted to do, whether it was art or sports, as long as I had good grades. My parents really pushed academics; everything else was secondary to that.

My mother is one of eleven children, nine of whom are girls. So I always had ample role models around me: strong, supportive women who stayed close and helped each other through the good and the bad. All of them have played mother to me at some point or another by giving me advice about a boyfriend or fashion choices, or school. My father arrived in America from Ireland with no evidence that he had an education, so he had to take any job he could get to raise a family here. I think I get my drive from him. He seized what was offered and proved that it doesn't really matter where you come from, it's where you're going.

I picked running out of curiosity. I had done everything else. I grew up in Allentown, Pennsylvania, playing every sport: skiing, softball, and other team sports. When I went to college I had to stop being a part of a team in sports. It was the first time I wasn't participating in something regularly, and I started to get really antsy. I had heard about disabled sports and wanted nothing to do with them. I had always competed against able-bodied athletes. I had never even met another amputee until I was a teenager. I thought disabled sports offered no challenge. But I couldn't have been more wrong. I didn't know the difference between the Special Olympics and the Paralympics. The Special Olympics are for people with mental disabilities and are about gathering self-esteem, but the Paralympics are for people who are physically challenged: amputees, people in wheelchairs, and people with cerebral palsy. The Paralympics are extremely competitive.

My situation is unique in that I had to create a market where there was none. Society's ignorance of disabled sports is incredible. Only 5 percent of the nation has even heard of the Paralympics and 1 percent of those think it's the same thing as the Special Olympics (whereas 70 percent of the nation has heard of the Special Olympics). When people interview you, you get the two-minute, feel-good spot at the end of the news broadcast: "Oh how sweet, she's a girl and an amputee who runs!" But I have pushed not to talk about myself as a disabled athlete. I am a strong woman with an attitude. I now get serious features in *Sports Illustrated Women/Sport* and great exposure because of my skills, not because I am missing legs. I am a world record holder in the 100 meter and the long jump, and a national record holder in the 200 meter. I am a world-class athlete and that's what counts.

I am starting to do modeling. I think it is important to show young girls the image of a healthy body as something sexy and glamorous. Women athletes have an inherent sense of pride and confidence. As an athlete, you have to be confident and poised—qualities you take with you off the track and outside of your sport. That's why you see so many female athletes with advanced degrees and accomplishments in other areas.

Women no longer have to trade their femininity to be treated seriously as athletes. Before Title IX twenty-five years ago, women who played sports were expected to become masculine to be taken seriously, much like women who first infiltrated the corporate world. Now, there is this wonderful celebration of women in sports and their strong, healthy bodies with muscles. We are now seeing role models like Gabby Reece and Steffi Graff in the *Sports Illustrated* swimsuit issue. To show an athletic woman's body as sexy sends such a positive message to the public. It's a wonderful example to show to our young daughters and nieces, our sisters and our cousins, especially with such a high rate of eating disorders among women. Women need to see people who take care of their bodies and are in the best physical shape they can be in.

Last year, women overtook men as the number-one purchasers of athletic gear. Women are stepping up to the plate. The male-dominated world is opening up. There are new professional opportunities for women in sports that didn't exist five years ago. We now have a semi-professional softball league, two professional basketball leagues, and the women's World Cup in soccer. There is a woman commentator for the

NBA playoffs. Title IX is greatly responsible for this and not enough can be said about the efforts of coaches and schools to accept women athletes and encourage their participation in athletics. Today girls grow up without the same limitations placed on them. They don't have to think, "Maybe I can play my sport through high school, or maybe get a scholarship to college." Now they can go all the way. They can grow up feeling good about themselves and with a positive outlook, which affects all aspects of their life. I can't wait to see what this generation of women, which has grown up in a sky's-the-limit atmosphere, will do in twenty-five years. I'm sure they will not only change the future of athletics; I'll bet they'll change the the world.

MOVING FROM BEING A FIGURE OF SYMPATHY TO BEING THE SUBJECT OF A MAJOR FEATURE STORY IN *SPORTS ILLUSTRATED* WAS AN INCREDIBLE VICTORY NOT ONLY FOR ME PERSONALLY, BUT FOR ALL DISABLED ATHLETES. IT IS IMPORTANT TO FOCUS ON THEIR TALENTS AND RECOGNIZE THEM AS ATHLETES FIRST WITH THEIR DISABILITY AS SORT OF A CHARACTERISTIC.

Funny things happen to me because I am an athlete who is missing legs. One of them was at the Big East Championships. I was running for Georgetown University as the first disabled person to compete alongside able-bodied athletes in the NCAA, so I was something of a novelty at these meets. I was in the 100 meter. It was the first time I had used the sprinting legs in hot weather; I had only had them for about a month. We didn't know what would happen to them when the climate changed. There is a silicone sleeve that holds the sprinting leg on, and when I started to sweat, the sweat acted as a lubricant. As I ran I started pistoning in my leg and at about seventy-five or eighty meters, I almost came out of my leg. It was the most horrific experience of my life. I was terrified because about a half an hour later I was supposed to run in the 200 meter with thousands of people watching. I went over to my coach and begged him not to make me run this race. My coach, Frank Gagliano, is a legend in track and field and has coached five Olympians. He is a big, intimidating man with a Brooklyn accent. I literally got down on my knees and begged him not to make me run, so that my leg wouldn't come off in front of all those people. But he was ignoring me. He looked at me and barked, "So what if your leg falls off? Ya pick it up, ya put it on, ya finish the goddamned race! Now get out there and run the duce." I was stunned that this man took no—for lack of a better

word—pity on me. I had proposed to him the worst-case scenario—my leg coming off, me falling in front of thousands of people—and he made it seem so simple. You pick up and you still go on—advice you can use pretty much anywhere in life.

I was invited to the Women's Sports Foundation Dinner at the Waldorf-Astoria, a big event for female athletes. There is something called the Grand March, and the emcee of the evening introduces to the thousand guests every athlete invited to participate. During the rehearsal for this, eighty-nine other athletes and I practiced marching up onto this set of bleachers. I was standing in front of Jeannette Lee (the "black widow"—an incredible billiards player), and we were joking that after the rehearsal, when all the women were getting hair and makeup for the real event that evening, I should ask for a pedicure. We were laughing mostly because we had been standing on these bleachers forever and were getting restless. Nadia Comaneci was standing behind her, and she didn't understand at first what was funny about a pedicure. I was wearing my cosmetic legs, which look real, and when someone told her that they weren't, she was stunned. When Nadia is stunned the whole room notices. It got sort of quiet for awhile, and I felt a little weird that my legs had caused a change in the atmosphere.

As I walked out to take my place that evening for the real dinner in a crushed velvet dress and strappy sandals, the emcee announced who I was and that I had been negotiating the bleachers on prosthetic legs. I received a long ovation from the crowd. I stood there basking in the attention, feeling incredible to be honored this way in the company of athletes like Billie Jean King. A few moments later Nadia leaned forward and tapped me on the shoulder. She said to me in this sort of campy voice, "Love the toenails!" I closed my eyes and thought, "This is one of those nights to remember."

i am often struck with the observation that the spirit of the young modern world is getting much more open-minded. because of the media, the boundaries between people—race, religion, handicap—are losing their tendencies to act as borders of the mind. what we gain is a more understanding, tolerant, and ultimately humane planet—a planet with a far brighter future than one in which we live apart, isolated, and fearful of our differences.

R I L E Y

team captain, america^3, america's cup, 1995

the only woman to compete in two whitbread races

On the drive from the airport in San Francisco, I wonder what Dawn Riley's office will look like. I'm shocked as we pull up to the airplane-hangar-sized building with seven-foot-high letters reading "America True." Dawn Riley, I realized, runs an empire. While I wait for her, I pick up a copy of her book Taking the Helm *and become duly impressed by her accomplishments as a sailor. She greets me in a suit and proudly shows me around her office. We head out to the marina in Dawn's old used van ("anything to save money for the race in 2000"). She kicks off her heels and squirms into shorts and a t-shirt while packing her brown-bag lunch. Someone calls on the cell phone—it's NASA with specs for the hull design of the new boat. Riley has $28 million to raise just to be able to compete in the America's Cup in less than two years; her life is a dichotomy of high tech and bare bones.*

I was born into sailing. I hate saying that because people always think that I was born with a silver spoon and a blue blazer. But my family did not have money; we did not belong to a yacht club. It's just something my family has done for years and loved to do. Sailing can be so many different things: you can be in a tiny little dinghy getting wet, in a little cat boat with a good old downy Maine sweater and a hat on, or on a huge luxury boat sailing into the sunset in your wealthy retirement. It's so diverse; that's what I really like about it.

The first boat my family had in Detroit, Michigan, was called the *Sieve*, because it leaked so much. My parents took me and my younger sister and brother sailing every single summer. We never had sailing lessons, so we went camping, canoeing, or whatever we could afford to do. My father made sure we sailed a lot whether we liked it or not. I remember catching my first fish—it was about two inches long. I was told to send it back because its mommy and daddy were really worried. Then I found out my dad hated eating fish so that was the end of my fishing career.

We used to cruise in the Great Lakes up in Georgian Bay and in areas around the North Channel in Canada. When I was thirteen we went on a year-long cruise. My parents had scrimped and saved for six years. My grandmother insisted that my parents could risk their own lives but not the lives of the grandchildren and that they should leave them home. Of course my parents laughed, but the reason she felt that way is because *Jaws* had just come out. But it *was* a crazy thing to do at the time, taking the whole family from Detroit and sailing down to the Caribbean and back. We went from Detroit out the barge canal; down the Hudson river; up to Maine; down to Florida, the Bahamas, and the Caribbean; to Grenada and back.

My father would always say, "Put down the book and trim the sail." But my mom was the one that put the plan in place to save for five years. She clipped out every single article you can imagine in preparation for the trip—from putting Vaseline on eggs so that they don't go bad to making cakes in a pressure cooker with no oven.

I did not go to school that year, but when I came back I got straight A's. Even though my schools and teachers were great, experiencing different things really brings history and math and science to life. I think that's why I'm so dedicated to True Youth—a nationwide educational program that creates new opportunities for young people—because I've seen the fruits of having an alternative experience. Although I definitely think that you need to have structured school. One year is about the maximum that I would want to take kids out of their environment. We did run into quite a few families that had been gone longer, say three to five years. The kids were really not able to socialize with other kids their own age—they were either really shy or really over the top. So I think a year is ideal.

BEING A PHYSICAL PERSON, AS A WOMAN, AND KNOWING HOW TO MOVE YOUR BODY, HOW TO HAVE BALANCE, HOW TO RUN, HOW TO TURN, HOW TO BE IN A CONFRONTATION WHETHER PHYSICAL OR MENTAL IS A VERY EMPOWERING THING. *it gives you a tremendous amount of confidence in everything you do.*

Somebody asked me to go racing the day that we got back from the trip. I realized that having all those sailing skills drilled in to me really paid off. I really got the experience to explode into the sailing scene and into the racing scene. Being a thirteen-year-old girl who looked pretty good in a bikini sure didn't slow me down either.

I planned on going into advertising in college. I had the option to go to the University of Michigan, which had a much better sailing scene, but I chose academics over sailing and went to Michigan State. (Our sailing team at Michigan State ended up being stronger when I was there after all.) We scheduled all our classes in the mornings so we could go sailing in the afternoons. On Wednesdays we would race to see who would be the top two skippers for the regatta that weekend, and then on Fridays we would pack up the boats and the car and drive anywhere from other parts of Michigan, to Indiana, Chicago, and Ohio. When I graduated, there were no advertising jobs to be had in Detroit.

So I worked on the boats down in Florida, having heard about an all-female team doing the Whitbread around-the-world race. I thought they were crazy, but as soon as I did a little bit more investigation I sent my resume over. I tried out, made the team, and became the watch captain in the first all-female, around-the-world race. And that was really cool because none of us had any hang-ups about whether we sailed with men or women; we just wanted people. As women we didn't usually sail with guys, unless we paid to be there or they needed a cook.

Most people thought that we would drown, or cry, or kill each other. It wasn't easy covering 32,000 miles of ocean. On top of the horrific weather conditions, there were other problems to solve. One night I was flipped out of my bunk when the boat rolled over forty-five degrees. Then I heard a huge bang. The wind slammed the rig down toward the sea, and *Heineken* rolled over onto her side in a violent broach. I got on deck as quickly as I could. With the boat on her side, no one could move easily—everyone had to hold on until finally she righted herself. Then there was an explosive sound and a "snap." We knew it was the rudder. The cockpit became a mass of spaghetti-like line from the abandoned spinnaker sheets no longer in use. It was nearly impossible to work on the boat. The waves were about thirty feet high and we were bobbing up and down with no sails pulling. The problem turned out to be a deteriorated rudder system. With 573 miles left to go, weather that was getting worse by the day, and no replacement parts, we had to do a makeshift repair job. I hacksawed a spinnaker pole to replace a rudder blade. It was an unconventional idea, but it kept us going until we could locate a replacement blade. Through sheer determination, we ended up coming in second.

There are such thrills in sailing. The America's Cup is internationally televised, and you sail in six-million-dollar boats that are on the cutting edge of technology. And it's close racing—you're fighting these boats one-on-one. Two boats line up, heading straight toward each other, and you basically play chicken. In the Whitbread, some of the thrills are surfing down a wave at thirty knots and slamming into the next forty-foot wave and continuing on at thirty knots. If it's dark or foggy, you head out knowing that there are icebergs out there that you're probably not going to see. You're taking your life into your own hands but at the same time making as many calculated risks as you can. On the flip side of that is taking as many safety precautions as you possibly can without slowing yourself down.

There was more than one time when I was supposed to be on a boat, and the owner was expecting Don Riley. When I get on the boat, they say, "Who the hell is that?" Most of the time they let me stay. And then they become born-again believers that girls can sail. As a girl I was not always allowed to participate, but I fought through that with the help of women and men—I think it's 50 percent up to the boys to encourage the girls. In kids aged ten to thirteen, I see total agreement and understanding between the girls and the boys. I see the girls lighting up about all the possibilities, and the boys being supportive. We should all be moving forward. There are plenty of other things out there to be concerned about without worrying about being boys or girls, men or women.

When I was growing up, I did a race at the end of every season called the Bikini Cup Regatta. The girls, wives, and girlfriends would sail the boat with no guys on board, except for one who would be the bartender.

I'M DOING ALL RIGHT. I FEEL PRETTY LUCKY. HOPEFULLY I'LL JUST KEEP DOING WH

I'M NOT STUPID—I WILL USE TO MY ADVANTAGE THE NOVELTY THAT I

BUT I HOPE TO GOD I NEVER EXPLOIT IT. IF IT CAN DO GOOD FOR OTHER WOMEN IN T

I'M NOT JUST A SAILOR, I'M ALSO A BUSINESSWOMAN.

The rules state that the skipper has to start and finish the race in a bikini, and at one point in the rest of the race everybody has to have had a bikini on. There's a contest after for the best male body and the best bikini. I was in the running for the best bikini prize one year and they took it a little more seriously, with a Miss America-like interview. They asked, "What do you want to end up doing with your life?" And I said, standing there in my bikini top and shorts, that I planned to be the first woman to steer in the America's Cup. As you can imagine, the guys laughed a bit. I have not reached that goal yet. But even if I steer for five minutes, I can say I've reached my goal. It will have taken twenty-two years, but I'll reach it.

WANT TO DO.

WOMAN,

ORT, ALL THE BETTER.

SHANNON

D   U   N   N

two-time world halfpipe champion
bronze medalist, olympic halfpipe competition, 1998
two-time u.s. open snowboarding champion

Shannon Dunn met me in Lake Tahoe, California, the day after Boarding for Breast Cancer, an annual fund-raising event she founded. BFBC is really the embodiment of the snowboarding community—which is giving and soulful—with thousands of people attending over the past two years. Shannon Dunn fit right in on the mountain, outfitted in full snowboard gear, including a snowboard emblazoned with a psychedelic drawing by Dunn herself. As we walked around the top of the mountain, Shannon was greeted by many women, and you never got the feeling that she was an unapproachable celebrity. She epitomizes what the modern athlete can be in a modern sport—enjoying it while she can and making the most of her ability by using her celebrity for the cause. As we wrap up the day, she joins her friends in a last run down the halfpipe. I watch them glide off as if on air, longing to follow behind.

Sports have always been a part of me. I'm short, and some people, when they see me, say, "I can't believe you're so little and you do all these crazy things." I don't know if they expect me to be some guy-girl or huge person. I never thought of myself as a tomboy—I'm just a girl who likes sports.

I grew up in Arlington Heights, Illinois, a suburb of Chicago. My family was very into sports. I did a lot of gymnastics and ice skating. My father was a semi-pro hockey player and owned a pro shop and an ice rink. He was also a hockey coach. My brother played hockey, and I really wanted to play too. I had a pair of little hockey skates, but there weren't any teams for girls and I didn't really want to play with the boys. I was too intimidated and shy. So I would play with my brother, whom I idolized. Anything he wanted to do I wanted to do. I would go to all his games and carry his big bag full of hockey equipment. I also went to a pretty good gymnastics academy when I was younger and I loved it. Mary Lou Retton was my inspiration. But we moved to Steamboat, Colorado, when I was nine years old, and there wasn't really a gymnastics program or an ice-skating rink. That was a bummer. Gymnastics and skating were my two very favorite things to do—they consumed me—and now I couldn't do them.

So I did a lot of activities with my dad and my brother—baseball, basketball, soccer. My dad would try to cheat with the score so that we could be even but I hated that. I got mad at him for doing that—I'm pretty stubborn. But my dad was an important influence on me as an athlete. He always talked about determination and the importance of a positive attitude. He can make anything sound good even if it's not. I like that though. I'm an optimist. I always think I can do something, no matter how crazy it might be.

I guess I was an athlete all my life, but I didn't really realize it until snowboarding came along. My brother taught me how and I used to ride with my friend Betsy. We were the only girls for awhile. I started going to contests with my brother although I didn't become a competitor until my junior year in high school. I didn't finish last, which surprised me because I thought I definitely would. The first time I tried the halfpipe I landed on my butt and bruised my tailbone badly. But it looked fun, and I wanted to learn. One thing led to another, and I was trying to get better and better with no particular goal in mind. So I don't think I picked snowboarding to be "my" sport. It just happened. I thought that I would stop snowboarding and go to school and have a "real" job. I wanted to go out into the business world, which is really funny because now that's the last thing that I want to do.

When snowboarding was new, you knew every snowboarder on the mountain. Everyone was so excited about it— it was such a different thing than it is now. People were doing it for no other reason but to have fun. Like skateboarding and surfing, snowboarding has character. It's a lifestyle. Every day it's nice to be up on the mountain. And it's awesome to ride on a mountain where no one has ridden before.

Although I was a little worried about "selling out" by competing in the Olympics, I was super-stoked to go. I was the first person that had to go down the pipe. People kept saying, "Oh, I can't believe you have to go first," and I said, "Oh, I don't care about it at all." It wasn't a big deal until I actually had to go. I was so stiff. I made it through without falling, but I didn't qualify. I had one more chance though, and when I went up to take my second run I thought, "Okay, I'm going to do this or I'm not going to make it to the finals." I ended up making it, but my goal in Japan was to have as much fun as I possibly could—because the Olympics might only happen once in my life—and I wasn't having fun. So I just turned things around. Once I started having fun, everything started flowing so well for me. When we took our final run I was in first place. I was having the time of my life, screaming my head off at the top. It was totally silent and serious up there and I just couldn't be like that. When I dropped in for my run, I said, "God, whatever you want to happen will happen. If I get dead last that's fine; if I get first that's fine. I just want this to be a good experience." For my second run I was doing pretty well and then I landed a trick and skidded out a little bit. When I got down to the bottom everyone kept saying, "I'm so sorry that you fell. You could have won." I couldn't believe that people thought that I would be upset, because I could have cared less. I had fun. I learned so much from that very moment. I don't ever want my achievements and my failures to affect my self-image. They should enhance you as a person.

You can make a good living snowboarding because it's the cool thing to do these days. It feels good to be on top of the sport as a woman because I've definitely had to push my way with the sponsors, promoting women and convincing people that a woman is a valuable asset to the company. Women in sports have to push a little bit harder for things they want to achieve. You have to work with the companies and make sure that you're not going to be overlooked. There wasn't always equal prize money for women in snowboarding and I used to just get irate. I would talk to the people who put on the contest—all the girls did. Now it's about equal. My marketability is just as good as the guys'. I've had to fight for that.

when you get to the

olympics, a sport loses

some of its innocence and

becomes commercial.

they want you to

wear a team uniform——

that doesn't really fit

with snowboarding.

i'm worried that kids will make winning a gold medal

their sole purpose. they'll miss the reason

the sport was created.

I think it's a successful person's responsibility to give back—to help others. My friend Tina and I are the cofounders of an annual event called Boarding for Breast Cancer. It was inspired by our friend in the boarding industry who died of breast cancer at a very young age. She wanted to generate awareness for breast cancer, so through the help of some really great people, we created this event, which has raised so much money. It's a great opportunity to be able to give back and promote a worthy cause.

WOMEN IN SPORTS HAVE TO PUSH HARDER THAN MEN FOR THE THINGS THEY WANT TO ACHIEVE. BUT YOU CAN'T LET SOCIETY'S BIAS GET IN THE WAY OF WHAT YOU WANT. THE SECRET OF MY SUCCESS IS TO FOLLOW MY HEART AND HAVE AS MUCH FUN AS POSSIBLE. THAT'S WHAT PULLS ME THROUGH THE HARD TIMES.

It's great for me to see snowboarding accepted for women and it has definitely come a long, long way. There are so many women riding now and so many great role models. It's really important for these athletes to promote a positive attitude in their sport. It's good for young people to see that. This is the moral of my story: if you can dream it, you can do it. You can achieve anything you want, not only in sports but in life. You just have to be a little creative. You have to ask the right people and keep asking and keep doing it.

CAMMI

GRANATO

olympic gold medalist, u.s. hockey team, 1998
three-time silver medalist, hockey world championships

Cammi Granato is very uncomfortable in the makeup and dress that I ask her to wear out on the ice. She worries that people will laugh. When she walks out the men instantly comment: "Hey Cammi, you gettin' married?" (we hear this one several times) or "Cammi, is that you, what's wrong?" The women, however, love the look: "Cammi, you look beautiful!" and "Cammi, show your legs!" She is then swarmed by the little girls who will soon pose with her. Someone's father approaches me on the side. His daughter Ariel had been teased so much that she quit the hockey team. He was hoping that Cammi would inspire her to rejoin. Another girl makes excuses for her pink shiny loafers to Cammi for fear of being too "girlie." Cammi and the girls unite on the ice. She entertains them with hockey tips and laughter. By the end of the day Ariel is ready to rejoin the team, and everyone wants to try on the dress.

There were six kids in my family, and we lived, breathed, ate, and drank hockey. My parents' first date was at a Chicago Blackhawks hockey game. We had season tickets to the Blackhawks and we went to all the games. We fell in love with hockey as a family. There was a pond across the street from my house—my brothers and sister and I would skate all winter. My mom wanted me to be a figure skater. That didn't really appeal to me, I guess, because when I was at the lessons, the minute my mom would turn her head, I would be off watching the hockey game at the adjacent rink. So she'd come and put me back on the ice, but the minute she would turn her head again I would be right back in the hockey rink. I guess she got the hint because she allowed me to sign up for hockey.

I played on my first team when I was six with my brother and my cousin. I can remember getting up at five o'clock in the morning, being so groggy, and my dad would dress me for practice. I had my long underwear on and he would put on my little shin guards, my socks, and my pants while I would stand and watch Saturday morning cartoons. Once I was dressed, we would be off to the rink.

The boys didn't think it was the greatest thing to have a girl on their team, but they learned in time to respect me because they realized I could help the team. But the parents and the people on the other teams needed convincing. Coaches from the other teams would say things like, "If she plays in this game she's going to get hurt, she's going to separate her shoulder. So tell her not to play." But I didn't separate my shoulder—that sort of thing didn't happen until I got a little older, when the guys got into checking and their egos got into play. Although one time I did get a concussion. I was hit from the side and knocked out, but I got right up because I knew my mom was there and I didn't want her to get nervous. After the game I was sitting in the stands and the kid who did it came up to me— he was near tears—and said, "I'm really sorry I hit you, my dad made me do it." I remember thinking, "Wow I really am crazy." I didn't understand why these parents were being so stubborn. I loved hockey. Why was it different

AT THE **OLYMPICS**, WE WERE TREATED LIKE

ELITE, PROFESSIONAL ATHLETES FOR THE FIRST TIME.

NOW THAT IT'S OVER, YOU ALMOST FEEL **CHEATED**. ON THE FLIP SIDE,

WE'RE GLAD WE GOT IT.

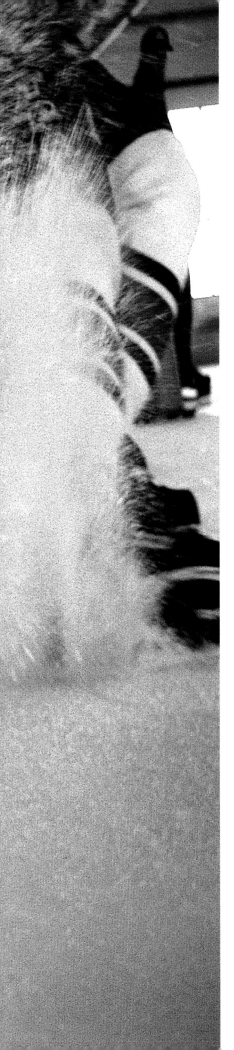

for me than for my brothers? Why were they allowed to be successful and not me? I couldn't get away from the fact that I was a girl playing hockey and not just a hockey player. I had to dress in the bathroom, and the girls watching and sometimes the parents would laugh at me as though I was doing something wrong. They would give me this look. It hurt my confidence. I felt very self-conscious when I walked into the rink carrying my bag. I knew that people thought I was crazy. But I'm glad I stuck with hockey, I'm glad I didn't listen to all those people.

My brothers have been my role models all through my life. I saw how much they accomplished and how successful they were in hockey. And I saw them become captains of their teams at Wisconsin in their senior years. They set the standard for me. When they got college scholarships I said, "If they can do it so can I." After playing only on boys' teams, then taking two years off, I joined a women's team for the first time at Providence College. So my brothers really drove me to push myself to become an elite athlete. And they still do. Tony has played pro-hockey for nine years, and I listen to him when he gives me advice like, "Don't deke, bury the puck."

At the Olympics, all the members of the team wore bracelets on our wrists. It's what we wore to symbolize our team. This bracelet was our circle and we didn't let anyone break it. We kept everything except the team out of the circle—the media, our families. We kept them out during the Olympics to make sure we were focused as a team. We had so much

power as one that we could accomplish anything we wanted. I never in my life saw a team pull together like we pulled together. No one got upset that she wasn't in a certain role—everyone just played and knew her job. We all pulled for each other and fought off each others' enemies.

In women's hockey there's heart and determination in every game. When men play hard in the playoffs, it's exciting to watch as a spectator, but I think women put that in every day. We're not used to playing for

IF I HADN'T WON
A GOLD MEDAL THIS YEAR
I MIGHT NOT BE ON THIS PAGE,
BUT I'D STILL BE ON THE ICE. *there are two cammi granatos. there's the well-kno*
and there's the lesser-known granato. the one who has happily cut up the ice since the a
through. but it's a labor of love. competitions are exciting but a player alone

ompetitive player

lieve, yes: this granato still sweats and goes through the same ordeal any other hockey player goes

e ice is something personal.

an entire season, so we don't take it for granted. This year, we got to be together for nine months, and it was like, "Well, I got to be a professional hockey player this year." Now that it's over you almost feel cheated. You think, well that was it, now I have to wait four more years to get it. On the flip side, we're glad we got it.

Being successful as a woman—and I think all women can relate to this—you're constantly pushing the door to get it open. Pushing with fists to get it open, gaining ground for everybody, for every woman. I'm really thankful that I was given a chance. You can't imagine how I felt when my brother Tony said, "Getting to see Cammi in the Olympics is probably my most exciting moment in hockey. She has gotten to a place nobody ever thought possible." Tony has scored thirty goals in a season four times in his career, but he still says things like, "She has surpassed me—she's not my sister. I'm her brother."

Being successful in sports has given me independence and strength. I learned that I can be strong and impressive on the ice, yet feminine off the ice. Younger girls are not going to have to go through the same things that we went though. It's great to know that I can influence kids in the right way, in a positive way. It's always rewarding to talk to kids. I've visited a lot of schools and I know my teammates have too. The kids really do look up to us, and it's fun to let them try on the gold medal, see the sparkle in their eyes, answer a question about their sport or what they're trying to do. It makes them feel important. That's what I consider success.

MASAKAYAN

two-time n.c.a.a. all-american
member, olympic volleyball team, 1988
inductee, u.c.l.a. hall of fame

When I first heard it, the term "beach volleyball" conjured up images of luxury and hedonism, sun and sand, independently wealthy people playing a game for fun. After meeting Liz Masakayan, I realize that it is the most physically challenging sport—jumping in sand takes its toll on your body, and Liz has had several surgeries on her knees already. It is also not a sport for those accustomed to stability. Most of her teammates hold two or three part-time jobs so they can travel around the world to compete. It's a sport whose time has not yet come—the 1998 women's beach volleyball doubles and four-person tours were canceled for financial and organizational reasons—but one which women have been instrumental in bringing into the limelight.

I was considered "the perfect child" who always got good grades and excelled in sports. That was my way of getting attention and love, although I didn't know that at the time. Luckily, I was gifted athletically so I succeeded in pleasing people by doing something I loved. I was brought up in a very competitive atmosphere. My brothers picked on me, so I was always challenged to be better than I was. Being the youngest meant I had to be ahead of my own age group in order to keep up with my siblings.

I guess I was a tomboy. I played little league baseball with the boys all the way through senior league. I made the all-star team when I was fourteen. The beach was half a mile away so I played beach volleyball all the time, and I also played soccer on all-boy teams. The other boys didn't really mind because I was a good player and bigger than most of them. But the parents got upset; the dads didn't want their sons to play with a girl. I guess I can understand their fear. They came from a different era and this was a new concept.

My mother was a very strong person. When I was five, we moved from the Philippines to Santa Monica, California, where she brought up four kids as a single parent in a two-bedroom apartment. My dad died when I was ten. I never really knew him. It wasn't an ideal situation, but I admire my mother for sticking it out and making it work. We didn't have much, but we learned to appreciate it. Because Mom worked so much, all the kids split the chores—we ran the house. I guess that's how I learned the concept of teamwork. She taught us to be disciplined, hard workers, and survivors. Mom gave us the things that mattered—love, time, communication. She made us strong, independent people.

Volleyball is the most challenging sport I've ever tried. The demands put on me—overcoming the difficulties of making my body do what it has to do so that I can succeed—have been my greatest teachers. The success of rebounding from injury and training to get back to full form is far greater for me than the success of winning a tournament or game. The payoff is, whether you win or lose, you still get to compete. And, you have to stay in shape for my job so I guess that's a perk.

If you work alone, like in tennis, it's all about you. In a larger team you can get lost with so many different personalities and how your personality compares with those of your other teammates. In volleyball, the success of the two-person team requires trust, responsibility, and problem-solving. I have learned a lot by having different partners and boyfriends, and there are a lot of similarities. There are always conflicts to work out and I am very much a person who likes to make things work. The key is to stay focused, play with confidence, and have patience. You can't worry about the score. Unfortunately, a lot of great athletes are so focused on winning that they don't really enjoy what they do or experience it in its fullest range.

a volleyball team

is a lot like a marriage:

it requires trust, responsibility, and problem-solving. it's an

intense bond you have with your teammate: you work,

travel and room together. and, as in any relationship,

there are problems that need to be solved. people

bring their own baggage to a relationship and if you

problem-solve fast enough so that these differences don't create

bitterness, you will have a

successful relationship. it's the same in volleyball. the ones who are

most successful are those who can problem-solve the fastest.

I'm very appreciative and proud to be a pioneer in our sport. I have been fortunate to have always been at the top of my game—that's not to say I started there, but it has been reasonably easy for me to stay at the top after working hard to get there. I am helping to build a foundation for women in sports and I am thrilled to be part of this changing and exciting time for women in athletics in the nineties. On the other hand, it is aggravating—to say the least—to be at the highest level in your sport, receiving all kinds of media attention and working as hard as men who are earning four times what you earn simply because they are men. Women's time has almost come in the sports arena in golf and tennis but in all other sports there is a huge gap between men and women. We have done our job and proven that we have great teams. In 1996 we won gold medals in gymnastics, soccer, softball, and basketball and now the hockey team did too. We just have to keep chipping away at the convention. We will get there.

WINNING IS NOT WHAT LIFE IS ABOUT. *my biggest attribute as a role model is not what i've won, but what i have learned about putting my life in perspective.*

SWOOPES

olympic gold medalist, 1996

member, u.s. national team with a historic 52—0 record,

1995—96

Sheryl Swoopes's number is 22, but her agent is toying with the idea of changing it to 23, Michael Jordan's number. There are a lot of similarities between the two as far as greatness is concerned, and both give each other the utmost respect. Sheryl even named her son "Jordan" in homage. There is one big difference that amazes me though. Sheryl returned to her former glory in the WNBA just six weeks after giving birth to her son last year. This is now a huge subject with her and her adoring fans, unlike the old days when professional female athletes had children and kept it quiet. Sheryl takes Jordan on the road with her, along with his devoted father, Eric, and somehow she manages to find the time to give her all to both of her full-time jobs.

When I went back to play for the Houston Comets six weeks after my son was born, there wasn't a single person I could talk to who had gone through that exactly. Other women who have had kids said, "It's going to take you at least a year to recuperate." But it wasn't about proving them wrong. I was doing it for me. I wouldn't do anything to jeopardize my health or my baby's, and if the doctor says, "Sheryl, you can't play anymore," then I won't continue to do what I'm doing. My number-one priority is taking care of my child. This wasn't something I planned— I didn't know it was going to happen. But now people can look at me and say, "Sheryl's a great mother and she still has her career."

I grew up in a single-parent home, and it was very difficult at times, because we didn't have the money to do things that a lot of my friends were able to do. My mother worked three jobs, and we sometimes needed public assistance. But even then, my mom was determined to give us all the things we needed in life and was willing to make the sacrifices that were necessary to achieve that. She wanted all of her kids to be the best we could possibly be. Her steadfastness and determination brought me to where I am today—she is the reason why I am successful.

It's funny that I ended up playing basketball because, growing up in Brownfield, Texas, I always wanted to be a cheerleader. I used to put on makeup with my cousin, cheer for my brothers at games, and even perform for the family. But I never tried out for the squad because we didn't have the money to buy the uniforms and pom-poms. So I began

MY NUMBER-ONE PRIORITY IS TAKING CARE OF MY CHILD. THIS WASN'T SOMETHING I PLANNED—I DIDN'T KNOW IT WAS GOING TO HAPPEN. BUT NOW PEOPLE CAN LOOK AT ME AND SAY, "SHERYL'S A GREAT MOTHER AND SHE STILL HAS HER CAREER."

to play basketball since my two older brothers played, using an old bicycle tire rim placed on top of a pole for the hoop. At first they didn't let me play, saying, "Sheryl, basketball is for boys." And when I did get to play, they were very hard on me, knocking me down and playing keep-away. But they were good teachers. Gradually, my shooting and drib-

bling got better. During junior high, I spent three nights a week playing hoops at the high school with the boys. I rarely got picked at first, and when I did, the guys almost never passed me the ball. And then they would humor me by handing me the ball and saying, "let her shoot." But all of this just made me work even harder. I learned that no matter what anybody tells me, as long as I believe it can be done, then I'm going to do it.

It is upsetting for me to hear about dads who tell their daughters they shouldn't play basketball and that they should be cheerleaders, ballerinas, or piano players instead. Girls need to hear that it's okay to play basketball or any other "boy's" sport and that they can be feminine at the same time. Kids used to call me a tomboy because I played basketball. They teased me because I had very long legs—they called me "Legs." But once I got older, I learned that I could wear makeup and dresses and still play basketball. It's okay to be on the court and be pretty. It's okay to be strong and shop at the mall.

BIG EGOS AND COMPETITIVENESS CAN BLOCK TEAMWORK—LUCKILY, THEY DON'T REALLY EXIST IN THE WNBA. NEITHER DO WOMEN WITH "ATTITUDE." THE COOPERATIVE SPIRIT AMONG THE PLAYERS IS NOT ARTIFICIAL—IT'S GENUINE. *as teammates we instinctively offer each other encouragement to achieve our mutual goals.*

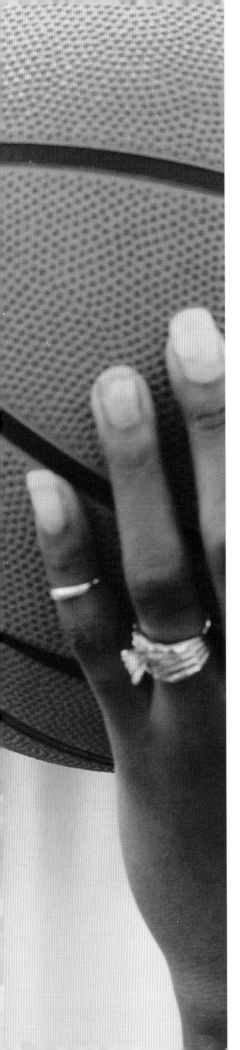

One of the best feelings I have ever had was at our first exhibition game at the University of Georgia. I saw a little girl smiling and waving at our team. She was wearing a red jersey. Number 7. "Swoopes" was on the back. I will never forget the sight—it was so gratifying and so moving that it caused a few tears to roll out of my eyes. I had seen my jersey in the store, but it was the first time I saw someone wearing one. And it still sends chills through my body to be the first female athlete to have a shoe named after her and to know that, all across the country, little girls will be going into stores and asking for the Air Swoopes.

STREET

olympic gold medalist, super-g, 1998

gold medalist, downhill, world championships, 1995

olympic silver medalist, downhill, 1994

It's blistering hot as I wait for Picabo Street to arrive for her portrait. I scan the crowd for this American sports icon, expecting to find her smiling and walking tall and strong. But Picabo arrives on crutches in obvious discomfort. We talk about what it's like to have come back from a terrible injury and achieve the ultimate in sports—an Olympic gold medal—only to sustain another disabling injury just weeks later. But this doesn't put a damper on her attitude: "I'm definitely going to compete at the 2002 games." Picabo has very definite ideas about things and puts her faith in a higher power. She draws strength from her belief that she has had previous lives that taught her about survival from the past. She is the ultimate combination of guts and cool: hippie parents, Cat-in-the-Hat name, generation X taste and intellect, rags-to-riches story, and the uncanny ability to come back after injury over and over again to steal the show.

I grew up in a small town in Idaho called Triumph, an old mining community with a population of about thirty-three. We had chickens and pigs in the yard and no TV. There were eight children in the entire town, including my brother and me; the rest were boys. I was a little tomboy, just trying to keep up. I wanted to do whatever my brother did, but I wanted to do it better. That's part of the reason why I have ended up where I am today. My brother is very athletic, and when he started to ski, I wanted to learn too. Since I wasn't old enough to go to the ski mountain, I started skiing in the backyard. I practiced for a good half year before I finally went to the mountain. When I got there, I did what I call a figure eleven—I went straight down to the bottom of the mountain. Everyone said, "You can turn, you know." And I asked, "What for?" The rest is history.

My parents were flower children. They didn't even give me a name until I was three. We were going on vacation to Mexico, and they realized I needed a name for my passport. They suggested "Picabo," the name of a southern Idaho town and the Native American word for "shining waters," and I nodded my head. My father, a brick mason, was a strict disciplinarian. When I was ten, I told him that I wanted to ski in the Olympics. So he pushed me as hard as he could and as much as I could take. There was an unspoken love in this intense push. My mom, a music teacher, balanced us out. She got shuffled around a bit because we were the tough guys who played her in the middle. But she was very patient. She was my safe place—and still is. When you're jumping so high for something so far up in the sky, you have to know that there is definitely someone there who can catch you, someone who knows how to catch you and when. Mom is just that way.

I became very adept at balancing energy in whatever form it came—be it positive or negative. You have to know how to handle the energy that's given to you and how to channel it positively. The energy may even come from your biggest competitor—if she gives you enough of that catlike, feisty-little-chick energy, you can say, "Come on, baby, give it all to me, 'cause I'll turn it around and use it to my advantage to do the best that I can do, and you won't even be a part of it anymore."

I think this attitude comes from my modest upbringing. We couldn't afford much, and my parents didn't have the means to buy the glamorous clothing and accessories that go with a sport like skiing. I was taunted by the rich kids on the slopes, which made me competitive and wild. Now, I feel that I've meshed my free-spiritedness with dedication—I feel no pressure from the outside because I apply myself. I create that pressure—therefore, I own it.

You play hard, you pay hard. Sometimes you're up and you stay up for a long time; sometimes you crash, then bounce up quickly; and sometimes you get slammed two, three, four times in a row—it's always an adventure. When you hear that another athlete has crashed, it takes a minute to catch your breath because you relive your own experiences. Before the 1998 Olympics in Nagano I had a bad crash in Sweden, just following a knee injury. People said that it would take two years to recover, that it would be a miracle to win in Nagano. Despite the adversity of the situation, it was a blessing in disguise. I had spent two years at the top, and the psychological strain was beginning to overwhelm my love for skiing. I needed a break to regain my excitement for the sport. The injuries gave me the chance to see clearly again. The training after my recovery was the most intense I've ever done, the most progress I've ever made mentally and physically. I was surprised to find out what a

INJURIES HAVE MADE ME RETHINK A LOT OF THINGS. YOU ALWAYS GROW IN DIFFICULT TIMES. YOUR LIFE MAY CHANGE, IT MAY NEVER BE THE SAME, BUT YOU LEARN MORE ABOUT YOURSELF THAN AT ANY OTHER TIME IN YOUR LIFE

strong person I am. That's why I say a higher power did this to me. I overcame the biggest stumbling block of my life and walked away with a gold medal. My sport has given me more ups and downs than any other avenue I could have taken in life. I think athletics do that for people. If you have the ability to concentrate on your sport and expand your mind and broaden your horizons amidst all that, you can really become quite an amazing person. It might seem backward—that you have to be an amazing person to do that. But it doesn't really matter, because it works.

My injuries have certainly made me rethink a lot of things. Because I've had to put some things on hold, namely skiing, I've been focusing on many new things that I wasn't interested in before and things that I wouldn't let myself think about before. It's amazing, too, just trying to become a healthy person again. Do that for the next year of your life and then we can talk about skiing. I have a new perspective on life. I am growing so much now as a person.

Winning the gold medal was my ultimate dream, and it became a reality in Nagano. I'm satisfied with what my sport has given me, but I'm looking for different lessons when I go back next time. I could stop right now if I felt like it, but I still want to go on. There's still a fire burning in me. I am planning to compete in the 2001 season and in the 2002 Olympics at Salt Lake City. After that point I will probably retire from skiing, and I'd like to get a TV talk show and become a motivational speaker. I really want to pass on what I have learned to others and help them to achieve the same kind of success that I have achieved. I want to help them over the hurdles and eliminate some of the mistakes that they encounter along the way. That's what I'm all about, moving people to be their best.

WOMEN IN SPORTS ARE NO LONGER
PIONEERING; WE'RE ESTABLISHED AS
A MOVEMENT AND WE ARE GROWING.
I'M PROUD TO BE PART OF THAT. *the next
step is to fatten the program and give all women
the chance to do whatever they want to do.*

LIPINSKI

Tara Lipinski is not only the youngest professional athlete I have ever met, she is also one of the most serious and dedicated. As I waited for her in the stands I watched her do her warm up on the ice, over and over again. Though she was practicing for an ice show, Tara took her performance as seriously as any major competition. She is a true perfectionist. It's no wonder that, at age four-teen, she captured the title of world champion, with an Olympic gold medal to follow one year later. Tara doesn't think much about being a successful female athlete; to her, it's just natural. Her only concern is competing to win. She's the living embodiment of what her predecessors have fought so long and hard for.

Skating has always been accepted for women, so I don't think I've done anything unusual, like women have in tra-ditional men's sports, such as soccer or hockey. I can't even imagine being confined to a career choice because of gender. I'm lucky—I come from a generation that doesn't question whether it's socially acceptable to do something or not. It's more a question of how well we do it. That's how I was raised. I just turned sixteen, so something like the King/Riggs match isn't even in my memory; it's just a part of past history. I hope that my legacy will be for young girls to know that they can achieve great things at any age if they work for it. Success doesn't have to be so far away. I want them to know how fulfilling it is to accomplish something you've only dreamed of.

When I was two, I climbed on top of an overturned Tupperware container and pretended I was receiving the gold medal at the Olympics. I had just watched a medal ceremony at the 1984 summer games on TV. I motioned to my mother for some ribbon and some flowers, and then I waited for the medal to be placed around my neck.

I started ice skating when I was very young. I started running when I was one, riding a bike when I was two, and roller skating when I was three. When I turned six, one of my mom's friends suggested to her that I try ice skating. My parents tell me that the first time they took me to the ice-skating rink, they remember watching me stumble and fall all over the place. They left for a second to go to the snack bar to get a cup of hot chocolate, and when they got back, they noticed that I wasn't falling anymore. I picked up ice skating immediately—I guess I was a natural on the ice.

ing; four forty-five-minute sessions on the ice; one session of ballet instruction (ballet really helps skaters make it all look easy); then four hours of schoolwork with three tutors.

FOR MY OLYMPIC LONG PROGRAM, I SKATED TO A SONG CALLED "RAINBOW." THE RAINBOW REPRESENTED MY HOPES AND DREAMS—EVERYTHING THAT I WANTED TO COME TRUE IN MY LIFE. *all through the program, i struggle to find the rainbow. when the music slows, i see the rainbow. i've beaten the storm, i can see my dreams. at the end, it's all mine.*

My mom doesn't push me. My coach doesn't push me. It's my thing. It's my skating—I love it and this is the best I can be. But my mom has had a huge influence on me. She has sacrificed so much to help me reach my goals. She's the one who told me to never give up. I owe it all to her. Both parents made a lot of sacrifices—we moved to the East Coast and then the Midwest so I could work with the country's best coaches. But my dad stayed in Texas to work. My family also had to take out some loans to pay for some skating expenses.

During competitions, I try not to think about the other competitors. If I skate clean, there's nothing else I can do. But I do get really nervous out there. I try to just think, "I want to do this." I think about the times I've skated well under pressure and I try to remember what that felt like. The most important thing for me to remember is definitely to trust myself.

A month before the 1997 Nationals, Coach Callaghan wanted to challenge me even more. He increased the difficulty of the combination jump in my long program. Instead of a triple salchow–triple loop jump, coach wanted me to try a triple loop–triple loop, a combination achieved in competition only once by a man and never by a woman. This means that I'd have to land the first jump flawlessly to execute the second. I landed it on my first try.

At the U.S. Nationals, I fell on my triple flip jump in the short program and dropped to fourth place. I knew it was a fluke, just a silly mistake. But that Saturday night, I landed seven triple jumps and the difficult triple loop–triple loop combination, I ended up winning second place overall. I remember just trying to block out everything and think only about what I wanted to do out there. You know, you have to forget about what you did before and just move on. That's one of my strongest points, I think—to look at a bad situation and come back strong from it and to prove to people that I can do something.

At the Olympics in Nagano, I wanted to win, but I didn't want to win so badly that it messed up my performance. I went out there and I tried to do it for the love of skating. I think that's why my program came out so well.

There's something that my mother and I do that I believe is really important. We usually visit a children's hospital together the week of a big skating event. It brings us back to reality. You really begin to think that life revolves around landing a triple lutz. You forget there is a world out there and people are living and dying.

Every day I wear a medallion representing St. Therese of Liseaux, "The Little Flower." She was the youngest person to enter the convent, fifteen, the same age as me. Everyone told her that she was too young, but her persistence proved her dedication. I make the nine-day novena prayer with my mother before competitions. I received the medallion as a gift from the mother superior of an orphanage in Corpus Christi, Texas. It really reminds me to have faith in myself, and it gives me spiritual strength that no amount of training can provide.

MULDOWNEY

the first woman licensed to drive a top fuel dragster

the first woman to win the u.s. nationals at indianapolis

the first three-time winston world championship winner

Shirley Muldowney has been racing for forty years. I first heard of her in my fifth grade reading textbook in the story "Lady Driver." I didn't know that she was still an active racer currently holding a world speed record. Shirley invited me out to her home in rural Michigan: "It's the one on the left with the white picket fence, rose garden, and the enormous dragster trailer in the driveway." Shirley is working in the garden when I arrive and Rahn, her husband, is working on "the car." It all seems typical enough until you realize that the car is a one-of-a-kind dragster that can climb to a speed of three hundred miles per hour in less than five seconds and that the lady in the garden is one of the most legendary racers of our time. Shirley is a paradox; in such a high-tech sport Shirley maintains an old-fashioned sensibility. She even hand-launders her own car parachute. She is enormously giving, wondering out loud how a young driver did last week and saying how worried she is about another one who will be driving at night for the first time—she hopes they remember the tips she gave them. While touring her office, I am amused by the hot pink decor (a Muldowney trademark) and impressed by the dozens of large trophies filling the shelves. There are pictures on the wall of Shirley with celebrity fans throughout the decades, including Madonna and Demi Moore. Also on display are the many helmets she has worn throughout her career—from the old speed-racer style, complete with goggles, to the aerodynamic Lady Diana memorial helmet, the yellow rose painted perfectly (Shirley is a great admirer). One in particular stands out among the shiny reds and pinks. It resembles a burnt, toasted marshmallow. "That one is from the fire," Shirley says matter-of-factly. "Young drivers need to be aware of the dangers. I'm always there to tell them." Given Shirley's long and unprecedented career, I'm shocked to hear how near to impossible sponsorship is: "No one wants to sponsor an old lady." I leave saddened by this. Shirley Muldowney has so much more to give.

I first saw the local hot rod while hitchhiking as a teenager. I would get rides to the outer limits of Schenectady, New York, to ride horses at the dude ranch where my father played in a Western band. Hitchhiking was more commonplace then than it is now, but it certainly wasn't the norm for a young girl. But I was already a daredevil. Thinking back on some of the rides I took, I'm pretty lucky to be here.

When I was in high school I got a job at a place called the Dutch Boy, a car-hop fast-food restaurant. It was there that I met Jack Muldowney. He was a member of a group of car enthusiasts called the Road Kings. My parents really liked him. I had always been a handful to them because I didn't listen, but they felt that I had some direction with Jack. So when I decided to get married at age sixteen instead of finishing school they allowed me.

Jack taught me how to drive, and I began racing when I was seventeen. I took to it like a fish to water. I loved the speed and sense of competition, and Jack, being an excellent mechanic, got quite a kick out of tuning the car that beat the boys. I would drive down Route 9 in a 1951 Mercury at 120 miles per hour with only a driver's permit. I raced on the street with a child in diapers at a time when I wasn't even old enough to drive after dark by myself. I had to get my dad—who was over six feet tall and 290 pounds—to ride with me when Jack wasn't available.

The male racers on the street would either verbally harass or ignore me. They used to let the air out of my tires during the night races. But I was a real tuffy. If you got in my way I was in your face. I knew it all. I had to be tough because I was on the receiving end. When I graduated to the fuel rigs and was touring the states, a guy from New York actually threatened me. He was a car enthusiast and a hit man for the mob, which I didn't know at the time. He didn't like me or the simple fact that I was becoming successful. I told Connie (Conrad) Coletta, who was a pretty tough guy in the early days. He straightened him out. Connie was the reason I left Schenectady, the one who inspired me to keep trying.

I started to move up through the ranks. I went from the Corvettes at the drag strip, to the door slammers in the various racetracks in the Northeast, to the dragsters, which was when I really began to get attention. I started to get involved in the National Hot Rod Association, and the newspapers started to fight for me and my rights as a woman. But they were also really hard on me in the early days—harder than on anybody out there, male or female. I was the only lady to drive a dragster fast enough to worry about. In 1965 I became the first woman to earn a license to drive a gasoline-powered dragster in an NHRA professional category. I spent the next four years on the match race circuit.

I started getting media attention when I went on tour. Jack, who didn't want to travel, started to pull back. Meanwhile, Connie and I got a little closer, which pushed me and Jack farther apart. In 1971, after touring all year without Jack, I left Schenectady and moved to Michigan to start a new life. The demise of the NHRA top gas class that

year also helped force a change in my career direction. I stepped up to the category of funny car and won the very first funny car race that I entered. These cars were run on very explosive nitromethane, with tubular fiberglass bodies. They were awkward looking, dangerous, and very difficult to drive. In the three years I spent behind the wheel of a funny car, I was involved in at least four bad fires caused by engine-part failure. In funny car racing, the driver sits straddling the motor, and when it comes apart, the oil and sometimes the fuel get on the red-hot exhaust pipes and ignite while the car is traveling at speeds well over two hundred miles per hour. The effect is like facing a blowtorch while driving at a speed equal to one football field per second.

THERE WAS NOTHING I WANTED MORE THAN TO BEAT THE BOYS.
BUT I PAID MY DUES AND CLIMBED THE LADDER SLOWLY,
WHICH IS THE WAY IT NEEDS TO BE DONE IN SUCH A DANGEROUS SPORT.

but i didn't do what i've done alone — i couldn't have.
i've been blessed to have had the constant support of so many talented people.
they keep me competitive while also keeping me safe.

One of my worst accidents was a fire in 1973, and I vowed that it would be my last. Following my recovery, I made the switch from funny car to the premier class of top fuel, the fastest of all cars. I quickly became the first woman to advance to the finals in top fuel and to break the five-second barrier. I am the first woman to become a member of the All American team. In 1976 I achieved one of my dreams: posting the best speed of the entire season (249.30). I was named Top Fuel Driver of the year.

In 1982, I became the only female to ever win the U.S. Nationals in Indianapolis—the granddaddy of all the races. The final round was the quickest, fastest side-by-side race in history, and I happened to race against Connie Coletta. I had been with Connie from 1971 until 1977. He was barred from racing because of a fistfight in 1972 and had become my crew chief. But I broke up with him at the end of 1977—the mental and physical abuse were far more than I could tolerate. He doesn't have great control over himself. In 1980 I started dating Rahn Tobler, who had taken over for Connie as crew chief. Rahn was only twenty-five years old, but he was already a three-time world champion as a crew chief—no one else has ever done that. We've been married since 1988.

I think the changes in the sport for women have been terrific, but the ladies have had to earn it. The truth is, there weren't many ladies in the early days because they were in the way and they were dangerous. They didn't have the experience and the know-how. I walked up the ladder piecemeal, which was the way it needed to be done in the old days because it was so dangerous and such a free-for-all. Unfortunately, I don't think the new drivers today are schooled long enough. People think I have this attitude because I want to be the only woman driver, but that's just not true. I've experienced the dangers firsthand.

Since I became known for auto racing, people started to romanticize the idea of a female dragster. Several years ago, they made the movie version of my life story, *Heart Like a Wheel*. My character had a Hollywood makeover. To me, she seemed too soft and mushy. After a tough race she would get up from the car as if she were getting up from the table at a dinner party. But overall, it was a good thing for the sport, especially for young girls who are curious about racing. It makes me proud to know that the barriers I've broken down and the doors I've opened up are actually documented on film.

GAIL
D E V E R S

two-time olympic gold medalist, 100 meter
holder of eleven championship titles
u.s. record holder, 60 meter

JACKIE
JOYNER-KERSEE

three-time olympic gold medalist
four-time winner, heptathlon, goodwill games
world and olympic record holder, heptathlon

When Jackie Joyner-Kersee was born, her family named her after Jacqueline Kennedy: "She's going to be the first lady of something," her grandmother said. She was right. Now in retirement, Jackie has just completed the last season of her brilliant fifteen-year career. She went out with a glorious victory in the heptathlon at the 1998 Goodwill Games—not really much of a shock, considering that JJK has been called "the greatest female athlete of all time." Bob Kersee would be the first to agree with this prestigious title. As a coach at UCLA, Bob recognized Jackie's track potential and convinced her to train for the heptathlon, now her greatest event. Two years later the two married. Athletic greatness runs in the family for Jackie: her brother, Al, won the gold medal in the triple jump in Los Angles in 1984, the same Olympics in which Jackie won the silver in the heptathlon. Al has said of their childhood: "I remember Jackie and me crying together in our old broken-down house, swearing that we were going to make it out." Coincidentally, Al is married to world-class sprinter Florence Griffith Joyner. Jackie's retirement is not an ending; rather, it marks the beginning of a new generation. I look forward to the day when a new star emerges from her JJK recreation center, but Jackie herself will be the proudest one of all.

People ask if my relationship with my husband, Bob Kersee, suffers because he is my coach. But when I'm on the track, I'm there as an athlete, not his wife. When we go home, it's strictly husband and wife, and that doesn't interfere with our relationship on the field. I mean, it's not like we have a fight at home and then come out here so he can tell me I have to run five miles. It's very professional. We respect each other. We laugh and joke and try to make it fun. We have more disagreements on the athletic field than we do at home, but that's the way it is with any coach and athlete. Bobby is and has been successful with men and women alike. He is a great motivator and has a keen eye for talent. I know he gets the best out of his athletes. He knows when to push and when to back off. He is very perceptive, and that may be why he is especially successful when coaching women.

In the beginning, when we were first married, people were very hard on Bobby. They would see him publicly make demands on me during training and call it wife abuse. For example, I came off the field during the 1991 world championships with an injured ankle and another jump just moments away. I was visibly shaken. Bobby said, "If it's not broken, tape it. You're going to take your last jump." People accused him of every kind of exploitation possible after this, but the fact of the matter is that this was a normal action for a coach to take during competition, but people expected him to go easy on me. When Michael Jordan's coach sends him back into an NBA finals game with a sprained ankle, it's a gutsy move by the coach and a display of Jordan's heart. When Bobby does that with me, because I'm a woman and his wife, he's considered abusive. But I think that things have changed a lot since then, and the world has become more accepting of the strength female athletes have. It's a good feeling to know that we've come far enough that I'm not thought of as some kind of doormat that wouldn't stand up for myself. Believe me, that's not my personality.

Growing up in East St. Louis, Illinois, I didn't have role models to talk to. When I go back home, there are kids who really look up to me, and I can just sit down with them and have a chat. I can give them something I never had. I tell them to follow their dreams and make certain they're enjoying what they do. It's important always to put your own happiness, not competition, first. And when a young girl says she wants to follow in my footsteps, I tell her she must make her own footsteps and find what it takes to make those prints so profound that others will want to follow in her steps. That's how we'll continue to make each generation better.

Though lacking in material possessions, my family never failed to provide me with an abundance of love and support. My mother died suddenly at the age of thirty-eight, when I was only eighteen. She was the one who planted the seed that, even though I was black and female and from a family for which nothing came easy, I could achieve great things in this world. She taught me that the key to success was to set goals, and not to be deterred by hardship or distracted by temptations. To this day, she remains my biggest mentor; whenever I make a move I think of what she would want me to do. I was given a basketball scholarship to UCLA. I graduated in 1985, which I consider my greatest accomplishment. The Olympics were fun, but it was more important to me to graduate from college.

My biggest physical hurdle is asthma. Some days, I'm just struggling to make it through. I'm allergic to grass, and pollen is a problem. Many foods can give me an asthma attack. Sometimes it's so bad that I see little white spots before my eyes. But I try not to use it as a crutch. If anyone ever tells me I can't do something, I set out to prove them wrong. I try to be the best at everything I do. It wasn't until I nearly died from an attack that I began to take my condition seriously. I started to think of my asthma as part of my training, and I had to attack it with the same commitment and discipline. I viewed it as a threat to my ability to continue competing in athletics, and I wasn't going to lose the ability to do what I most enjoyed just because I was stubborn. I had to learn to control the disease instead of letting it control me. If you don't, it will take you out of the game permanently.

Gail and I offer each other support through our ups and downs. As athletes who live with ailments that can hinder our performance at any time, we both understand each other's discipline and try to stay as fit as possible without ignoring our symptoms. We give each other words of encouragement through the difficult times.

The JJK Community Foundation gives out grants and scholarships. We are planning to open a recreation center in my hometown for the fourteen thousand youths in the community. It will have basketball courts, a track, a swimming pool, baseball and football fields, and educational facilities. When I was growing up, I developed my athletic skills at the Mary Brown Center. I used the library, I learned crafts, I was a cheerleader, and I did modern dance. The center has since closed, and I want to be part of a facility in East St. Louis that can develop the same kinds of opportunities for youths. When I leave this earth, I want to know I've created something that will help others. I want young people to look beyond the things I have done on the athletic field. I never envisioned being asked for my autograph or being on magazine covers. All I ever wanted was to do my best. I am proud to be a role model not just as a black woman, but as a woman. We have made great strides, but there is still a lot more to achieve.

The day we meet, Gail Devers, the 100-meter gold medalist from the 1996 Olympics, is training for the Goodwill Games with her friend and training partner, Jackie Joyner-Kersee. An amazing athlete, Gail has returned to champion status after being diagnosed with Graves disease, an ailment that brought her within two days of having both feet amputated. Her recovery was nothing short of a miracle. It's the middle of a record heat wave in St. Louis and their coach, Bob Kersee, is upholding his reputation as a very serious and focused trainer. Despite the heat, they train as usual, both enduring a grueling four-hour workout, track and field exercises, and weight training. I set up my camera to catch Gail in action. I had never shot track and field stars before, and I waited for the right moment to click the shutter. It was amazing how fast she would fly out of frame. She was poised and courteous, if slightly camera-shy. It was clear that, despite her fame and notoriety, she is very grounded in her identity. Gail Devers will undoubtedly continue to break records for years to come and continue to represent what role models are all about.

In 1988 I began to suffer vision loss, wild weight fluctuations, migraine headaches, sleep loss, fainting spells, fits of shaking, and nearly perpetual menstrual bleeding. I fought hard for two years but the disease overpowered me and I had to stop running. Deep down inside, I was scared to death that I was finished as an athlete. I was finally diagnosed with Graves disease, a rare thyroid disorder. But the radiation that doctors used to destroy a cyst and the bad part of my thyroid gland destroyed the whole gland. My feet began to swell and ooze, and my skin cracked and bled. The pain was so bad my parents had to carry me to the bathroom. My feet were so blistered and swollen that the doctors said they were within two days of amputation. Then they realized that the radiation treatments might have been to blame. The therapy was changed, and in a month I was able to walk. I started to walk around the UCLA track in socks. Two months later I was hurdling. Three months later I won the silver medal at the 1991 world championships in Tokyo, and then I won the gold medal at the 1992 Olympics in Barcelona. I feel like I have a guardian angel looking over me. If I keep the faith, nothing bad can happen.

I was raised in San Diego in a Leave-it-to-Beaver family. My father is a Baptist minister and my mother is a teacher's aide at an elementary school. We had picnics, rode bikes, and played touch football. We did Bible studies together. My brother, Parenthesis, and I used to have running races. He would make fun of me when he won. One day I decided I wasn't going to lose any more, and I started practicing on my own. The next time we went out, I beat him and he never raced me again. Instead, he would get his friends to run against me. I beat them too. My brother was like Don King. He set up match races between me and other kids in the neighborhood. I think he was making money off it. My brother and his friend would ride bikes and I would run alongside them. I was too shy to join the track team in high school, but my brother insisted. From then on, running was all that mattered.

BEFORE EACH RACE, I RECITE LUKE **11:9** BECAUSE IT MEANS SO MUCH TO ME. "ASK AND YOU SHALL RECEIVE; SEEK AND YOU SHALL FIND; KNOCK AND IT SHALL BE OPENED TO YOU." FAITH IS A POWERFUL ENERGY BOOST. WHEN YOU ARE GOING THROUGH A ROUGH TIME IN YOUR LIFE, YOU HAVE TO BELIEVE YOU'RE GOING TO GET THROUGH IT, THAT YOU CAN GET THROUGH IT. IT HAS TO BE YOUR DAILY PRAYER.

The word "quit" isn't a part of my vocabulary. I love the sport and I want to continue to excel. I think that my best is yet to come. When my career in running is over and I can dedicate the valuable time needed for a "hands-on" commitment, I'd like to open a learning center. I always wanted to be an elementary school teacher. I used to turn summer babysitting jobs into impromptu summer school, using my mother's teaching materials. I believe that life is a learning experience. I think what I've gone through can help others.

our hope for the future

is that women's sports continue to excel:

that the little girls who come after us

will have even more benefits than we did:

that laws will not be necessary to make the playing fields equal:

that power, grace, and the elegance of women's performances in sports

will be as recognized in the daily headlines

as michael jordan, mark mcgwire,

or any other great male athlete.

What is it that defines a true athlete?

What is it that makes female athletes unique?

What is it that separates world-class from average?

These are the ideals presented in *Women Who Win*. The fine athletes in this collection were chosen not only for their accomplishments in sports, but also for their pioneering spirit in fields otherwise dominated by men. It's amazing to think that the women's basketball leagues are only in their beginning seasons and that the women's soccer team is about to compete in its first World Cup. The hockey team, without a league of its own, has just won gold at its first Olympic games. Not so long ago, there was no ABL and I had to play abroad in order to live my dream of being a professional player. Like many of the stories in this book, mine is one of persistence, devotion, and sacrifice—qualities that characterize professional female athletes.

Overall, these are stories of celebration—what makes a woman and her athleticism endure and evolve. These could have been stories of anger and frustration, but they are not. Instead, they are stories of strength: the power of leadership in the face of adversity; the importance of mentors, role models, and people who give children the boost they need to rise; the inescapable influence of our parents.

The athletes in this book are women who shape their own existence, their own goals—they teach us what true sportsmanship is all about. It is humbling to think about the women who have come before us, born into difficult circumstances and conflicting expectations and told to live inside the boundaries. Yet somehow they bravely went outside them, rewriting the assumptions and conventions that told them who they should become.

As an athlete, it makes me proud to think that the story I share with other women in sports will ultimately bring inspiration and satisfaction to the lives of others for years to come.